Superwoman
Jacqueline Cochran

Family Memories about the
Famous Pilot, Patriot,
Wife & Businesswoman

by

Billie Pittman Ayers and Beth Dees

© 1999, 2001 by Billie P. Ayers and Beth J. Dees.
All rights reserved.

No part of this book may be reproduced, stored in a retrieval system, or transmitted by any means, electronic, mechanical, photocopying, recording, or otherwise, without written permission from the author.

ISBN: 0-75966-763-2

This book is printed on acid free paper.

1stBooks - rev. 10/18/01

This book is dedicated to
the loving memory of
my mother and father
Joseph Edward and Ethel Pittman
to my sisters: Gwen and Bennie
and to my brothers: Gordon, Joe and I.D.

                        Billie P. Ayers

This book is dedicated to my family and
husband, Marc.

                        Beth J. Dees

Table of Contents

Chapter One:	Fast Departures, Smooth Arrivals	1
Chapter Two:	Never-Ending Sawdust Roads	12
Chapter Three:	The Unknown from Noma	20
Chapter Four:	The Phoenix Flies	39
Chapter Five:	Jackie goes Solo	47
Chapter Six:	Gwen's Bird's Eye View	56
Chapter Seven:	Paradise in the Desert	65
Chapter Eight:	The Bendix …Super bowl of the Air Races	76
Chapter Nine:	Jackie, Amelia Earhart and ESP	84
Chapter Ten:	Queen WASP in WWII	100
Chapter Eleven:	Eisenhower and LBJ's Sunday Visit	121
Chapter Twelve:	Yeager's mission: Save Jackie from Jackie	132
Chapter Thirteen:	Smooth Landings	147

Foreword by General Chuck Yeager

"...Jackie's record [of breaking the sound barrier was my project, I was her teacher and chase pilot. I first met her in 1947, not long after I broke the sound barrier, in Secretary of the Air Force Stuart Symington's office. She was a tall, blonde woman in her forties. "I'm Jackie Cochran," she said, pumping my hand. "Great Job, Captain Yeager. We're all proud of you." She invited me to lunch, acting as if I should know exactly who she was, and caused an uproar just entering the posh Washington restaurant. The owner began bowing and scraping, and the waiters went flying. During the meal she sent back every other course, complaining loudly, and even marched into the kitchen to give the chef hell.

"In between pumping me for all the details of my X-1 flights, I learned a little about who she was. She was a honcho on several important aviation boards and committees and was a famous aviatrix before the war, winner of the Bendix air races; she had been a close friend of Amelia Earhart's During the war she was…in charge of the WASPs, the Women's Air Force Service Pilots ... Hell, she knew everybody and bounced all over the world: on VE Day, she was one of the first Americans to get down inside Hitler's bunker in Berlin, and came away with a gold doorknob off his bathroom by trading for it with a Russian soldier for a pack of Lucky Strikes. On VJ Day she was in Tokyo, playing poker with a couple of generals on MacArthur's staff and conned her way on board the battleship *Missouri* to watch the surrender ceremonies. As I would learn more than once over the next couple of decades, when Jackie Cochran set her mind to do something, she was a damned Sherman tank at full steam."

> [Excerpted with permission from General Yeager's autobiography]

Preface

I already knew of my Aunt Jackie's death on August 13, 1980 when the news appeared in national newspapers. Though my family's contact with her had been infrequent since the early 70's, a family member had called to tell us the sad news. I read with pride of her long list of accomplishments, but there was a sadness too because I also read the untrue information reprinted about her early life. Over the years my concern increased that she never let the world know why she reinvented her early life story. The reasons are complex. Jackie was complex.

Until now, the family has always kept quiet about the true events surrounding Jackie's birth and early years. We loved her. We still do. We didn't want to upset her life. We all have secrets that can be a tremendous load. To release the pressure sometimes one must open up and share them.

Jackie was a great person to me. Not because she became famous, knew U.S. presidents, movie stars and many important people or because she accomplished so much for aviation, but because she was a loving, generous and energetic member of our family. She positively influenced—and still does—many lives, yet Jackie was human and made mistakes like everyone else including myself. The family memories and facts I bring out in this book are told to fill in the blanks, to enhance the story already known about her life.

Along with other family members, I feel it is time to tell the true story of Jackie's early life—to set the record straight. Why? We feel it is important, for the sake of our family and history, that we document our memories, our knowledge about her early life. Also, I believe telling the true story of her early life will set her spirit free to soar, relieved the truth is told. I fear she may have missed the true peace and happiness we all seek because she was unable to faced and forgive herself for her actions as a young woman. She may have reinvented her early life story give herself anonymity, or perhaps she felt it would make her story more interesting. My aim is to bring out the thread of Jackie's early life and show how it weaves through her entire life, a life of great accomplishment. It is my hope this story will offer more insight into one of the greatest women flyers and personalities of all times—Jackie Cochran.

Billie Pittman Ayers

Billie and I enjoyed several years together working on this project and when we had finished the manuscript she died suddenly of a stroke. I've honored an agreement we made to tell her story and I am pleased, with the help of her daughter, Vicki Ayers, to accomplish a goal of Billie's and mine of getting this project into print where it can be shared with others.

Beth J. Dees

Acknowledgements

I wish to acknowledge Beth Dees who helped me research and write this book. She first knew of my Aunt Jackie from living in DeFuniak Springs where she heard stories from the residents there about her. Her persistence, interest and great admiration for Jackie enabled us to get the story told.

I wish to acknowledge my sister, Gwen, who passed away March 18, 1977. She and Gordon, my younger brother and I decided in the late 1970's to write this story. We asked Jackie's cousin, Pinkie Grant, a writer with *The Mobile Press Register*, who also worked in radio and TV, if he would help us with the story and he said yes. He too has since passed away.

My husband, Mose, has been very patient and supportive of this project, which has taken so many years to accomplish. My daughter, Vicki, has always encouraged me and has helped in many ways; typing, listening, reading to me when my eyes bad, going with me to Tallahassee, along with my nieces, Carolyn and Sharon, to accept a plaque from Governor Childs upon Jackie being inducted into the state's Commission on Women.

A special thanks to General Chuck Yeager who allowed us to use excerpts about Jackie from his autobiography *Yeager*. He has always been a loyal friend to Jackie and to Floyd and, he knew her better than just about anyone, which is why I appreciate his letting us use what he thought of Jackie in his own words

There have been so many others who were friendly and helpful. Among them: Dean DeBolt and Katrina King of the University of West Florida Library. Tom Brannigar and Hazel Stitt at the Dwight D. Eisenhower Library. Harold Gillis and Jeannette MacDonald of DeFuniak Springs were particularly helpful in sharing articles about the area and helping Beth and I to find the folks to interview. Drina Abel, a true wing-walker and admirer of Jackie helped direct our early research efforts. I was amazed and helped by information from Melanie Howell a young Pensacolian who chose Jackie as her project study subject and won prizes for it. I appreciate the dozens of friends and family members I spoke with who gave of their time and memories.

                                Billie P. Ayers

Disclaimer

This book is written to share the memories of Billie Pittman Ayers about her Aunt Jackie Cochran. It is not a biography. There is much information documented about Cochran and the bibliography references many excellent sources. The purpose of this book is to educate and entertain.

Every effort has been made to make this manual as complete and as accurate as possible. However, there may be mistakes both typographical and in content. If you are aware of an error, please email Bjdeez@aic-fl.com.

SUPERWOMAN Jacqueline Cochran

Chapter One: Fast Departures, Smooth Arrivals

Jackie watched the daylight fade in front of her even though it was just after noon. On the 21st of May, 1953 the stars came into view as she piloted the F-86 Canadian-built Sabre Jet away from earth into the thinning atmosphere. The serene dark blue skyscape was lost to the pilot as she focused on the spinning dials, red and green glowing dots and fast flowing numbers on the instrument panel in front of her. Outside the temperature was frosty. Inside Jackie sweated in her anti-gravity suit, customized to fit her female contours. About eight and a half miles above ground, she pushed the joystick forward. Within seconds her jet gently nosed over. She put it through a split "S" maneuver to begin the almost vertical, full power dive back towards the target of earth. Easing back the joystick, Jackie let all 12,000 of the engine's horses build to a full run. It didn't matter the altimeter needle was spinning too fast to read; Jackie's eyes were on the Mach meter. It was Mach 1 she was after. Mach 1—the speed of sound.

"I counted the changes in the Mach Meter aloud over my microphone so Chuck Yeager could hear me in his plane," she recounted later. Major Yeager was one of Jackie's closest friends and six years earlier had been the first man in the world to fly faster than the speed of sound. Jackie intended to be the first woman. She saw herself as a female Daniel Boone of the air, going ever faster, higher and farther in her explorations of it. She considered breaking the sonic barrier an inevitable personal goal. A dream she meant to make happen.

Yeager was right beside her—literally—just off her left wing—in another F-86. Yeager had warned Jackie about the rough ride she would get when she neared Mach 1. His words proved true during trial flights earlier that week.

Later Jackie said, "As you start getting closer to Mach 1—you know, .97, .98, .99, there is a terrific turbulence. The wings start digging under. First one wing will twist and then the other, then another part of the plane ... then another ... all seem to be twisting and digging independently."

Silent seconds crept by in the cockpits as the pilots concentrated on flying their crafts. No time for chit chat. The flight would be over in a matter of minutes. The conditions were right for Jackie to see shock waves, created by the jet's breaking through the sound barrier, roll like a fine film of water off her canopy. Flying 651 miles per hour, Jackie's rough ride suddenly smoothed into silk. Crossing the sky faster than an echo through a canyon, Jacqueline Cochran became the first woman ever to break the speed of sound. The stars disappeared behind her as she flew back into the bright face of Earth. The sonic booms from their jets rolled many miles through the California desert below. It wasn't Jackie's first dream accomplished, or her last. It was only the 21st record of the total 120 she was to accumulate in her 40 years of flying. More than any pilot—male or female—held. Jackie knew how to make her dreams come true.

Forty-seven years before Jackie's historic flight, my grandmother, Mary Grant Pittman, called Mollie, wrote "Bessie Lee Pittman" using a dull pencil at the bottom of a list of names and dates on a small piece of paper. Bessie was my Aunt Jackie's real name. Beneath the name Grandmother Mollie wrote "May 11, 1906." Bessie was the youngest, my grandmother's "baby girl", of the five children born to her and Ira Pittman My grandparents lived in Muscogee, Florida when Bessie was born. It's only about 35 minutes from Pensacola, where I live now The Pittman family cemetery is only a few miles from Pensacola, just off County Road 64. Even then, Muscogee was a small community, a sawmill town, located near the east bank of the Perdido River. The second story of the mill had a large room where everyone gathered for business meetings and social dances. The local school sat up on a hill nearby. Despite its small size, the school with grades one through 12, had the distinction of sending more students on to college than any other school in the state. The school shared the hill with a Presbyterian church and a hotel. The Methodist met in a church next door to the mill's company store. There were the necessary businesses of all small towns: post office, barbershop, butcher shop, plus the mill commissary and the train depot. An artesian well sprang up, literally, in the center of town. Muscogee was near the slightly larger populated community of Gateswood, Alabama. The Perdido River snaked between the two communities with Muscogee, Florida. on its east bank and Gateswood across the river, westward about 20 miles.

Most of the men in Muscogee and Gateswood worked for the big Southern States Lumber Company. My grandfather, Ira, had a good job as a millwright there making slightly better money than the average mill worker. Millwork was a family tradition for the Pittmans in the early years and just about everyone else since it was about the only line of steady work available in the rural South in the late 1800s, early 1900s. Grandfather made a living for his family during a time when having the basics of food and clothing was not to be taken for granted.

The Pittmans, like the other mill families, may have been poor, but they didn't know it. To mill families, "poor" meant, not so much the lack of food or clothes, as being in tough straits without neighbors, family and or friends to help.

'Getting by' meant growing your own food and buying new shoes only when the old ones were worn out. My grandparents, like my parents after they married, had their own gardens, and chickens. They had enough to eat and shared with their neighbors when needed.

There were a number of neighboring families, the Peaglers, Irwins and Morris's who also earned their livelihood from the lumber mills. One neighbor, Erma Peagler was with my Grandmother Mollie when Bessie was born. There were no problems, which was good. Doctors were expensive and not always nearby when you needed them. Before Bessie, the family lived for a time in a converted train box car in Gateswood so they could easily be moved from site to site in the forests while the work of cutting down pines went on.

It wasn't an easy life living in a lumber mill community, but family made it better. Grandmother Mollie religiously believed in families and neighbors helping each other. It had to do with survival and it had to do with Love. Community made Life's offering of births, its takings by death and everything between easier.

This lifestyle of bare subsistence among rural families throughout Northwest Florida and the South seemed ironic because they were surrounded by something the world clamored loudly for—Yellow Long Leaf Pine. This almost solid hardwood was the preferred wood for construction. Virgin forests of trees, more than a hundred feet tall, with branches forming miles of a continuous green canopy, were desired for their precious lumber by a world just emerging from the devastation of World War I. But the Yellow Pine meant gold only for a handful of individuals who bought the land, owned the equipment and started up the lumber mills and turpentine stills in these virgin forests.

After the turpentine had been drained from the trees and all the trees had been felled, debarked, cut, planed, dried and shipped out as lumber, the mills would close and move because the forests were gone. The owners would shut down the millworks and move them to new forests and start operations all over. Working for a mill was the adult version of the child's game of musical chairs. When a mill shut down, everyone scrambled, looking for work and a new place to live. This meant uprooting the family and moving—across the river a few miles or across the state line a few hundred miles. Dozens of busy towns and communities where the Pittmans lived, like Bagdad, Millville and Paxton in Northwest Florida sprang up because of a new mill opening and often, after the trees were gone and the mills closed, these towns would slide into economic stagnation or decay and sometimes disappear.

Moving around so much meant doing without a lot of possessions. One of my Grandmother's prized possessions was the family bible. She had several through the years and I have one of her older ones with its cover missing. Bibles were more than just spiritual guidebooks. They contained legal records of a family's births and deaths. Like most folks living at the turn of the century in the rural backwoods of Florida, as far as I know, my grandparents didn't take the time or go to the trouble to obtain a birth certificate for their newborns. If it was written down in God's Word, that was enough. Until 1915—legally—it was. Mothers brought the family bible to school to register their children for school. Old people applying for Social Security benefits showed up with the King James' Bible under their arms. Florida legislators passed a law requiring birth certificates in the late 1800s, but it wasn't until they strengthened the law in 1915 that doctors and midwives began filling out birth certificates as required. That age-stained, permanently creased list of births written out by my Grandmother Mollie ended up in my Mother's bible.

Mollie and Ira Pittman's large family began in Gateswood with two boys. Joe arrived on May 29, 1894. Two years later Henry was born. In 1900, Mollie gave birth to the first of a trio of girls. Mary Elbertie, born January 5 was called "Mamie."

Probably to take advantage of a job change, Ira then moved his family 20 miles east, back across the Florida state line to Muscogee. While my grandfather went daily to oversee the condition of the mill's machinery, Grandmother Mollie took care of Joe, Henry, Mamie and their home. In 1903, a second girl—Myrtle Maybelle Pittman was delivered, the same year Orville and Wilbur Wright made their first flight in Kitty Hawk, N.C.

Three years later on May 11, 1906, Bessie Lee Pittman was born. She changed her name later to Jackie and she grew up to be the greatest woman pilot in the world.

Bessie may have been the 'baby' of the family for the rest of her life but she learned to deal with fear early. As a child, I heard this family story many times and always marveled at her bravery. She had been to visit some little friends and she was on her way home. It was already getting dark and of course she had been told ghosts or 'haints' lived in the little cemetery she had to pass. When she got close she actually saw one. She made a decision there she said that changed her life. Rather than running away, she ran at the ghost and it turned out to be a poor calf with its leg caught in some boards. After that she said she found it was easier to face her 'haints' than run away from them.

Years later my Grandmother Mollie would tell a newspaper reporter how shortly after Bessie's birth a fortune teller had accurately predicted her new baby girl's later fame, riches and many great accomplishments. All of it came true. What the palm reader didn't tell my proud grandmother was her baby would one day tell the world she was an orphan and deny the thing her mother held most dear—family.

Bessie's father Ira B. Pittman and mother, Mary Grant, called "Mollie." Ira was known for his quiet ways while Mollie was considered a strong personality. Mollie and Bessie were often at odds throughout life perhaps because of their similar personalities.

Bessie's oldest brother, Joseph E. Pittman, with his wife, Ethel Mae Ingram. Jackie lived with the couple and their children on and off during her young adult years.

Bessie's brother Joe stands besides Henry "I.D." Pittman. Though the reason in unknown, Henry had a crippled foot from birth which may explain his sitting position here.

SUPERWOMAN Jacqueline Cochran

Publicity photos of Jackie (far right) as a child consistently use this photo, except her two older sisters, Myrtle Maybelle (far left) and Mary Elbertie, called "Mamie," are consistently cut out.

Billie Pittman Ayers and Beth Dees

Chapter Two: Never-Ending Sawdust Roads

Today Bagdad is a small, quiet, southern town replete with historic homes and a restored downtown. At the time, Bagdad Land and Lumber Company was bustling, shipping out more yellow pine than any mill in the entire country. The owners—Joseph Forsyth and the Simpson brothers—picked the area because of its natural quality juncture between Pond Creek and the Blackwater River, which emptied, into Pensacola Bay. Schooners picked up the fine lumber and sailed out into the Gulf of Mexico and out to the world to deliver it. Bagdad Land and Lumber Company employed more than 1,000 men in its heyday and in 1912 that workforce included my grandfather. Joe, my father, had gone his own way to see the world as a sailor. In the early 1900s, my grandparents and their children lived in Pensacola while my grandfather worked in nearby Millview.

Though it seemed symbolic when Aunt Jackie wrote later in life of being "a refugee from sawdust road," she meant it literally. Such sawdust roads connected Bagdad, like many other mill towns. They were everywhere. The low areas along the bodies of water needed to transport the logs, easily became boggy and flooded. A mule and wagon carted around leftover chips and sawdust to spread over the dirt roads to keep them passable when it rained. There were no paved roads in any of the smaller communities.

One Bagdadian I talked to, Jewel Abel, was 16 years old when she began working in the front offices in the commissary at the Bagdad mill. For more than a decade, she did everything from filing to handing out coupon

SUPERWOMAN Jacqueline Cochran

books. She was proud of her job. After all, Bagdad Lumber Mill was the second largest and most progressive mill in existence. Even though the average mill worker's pay was low, only about $1 a day, Miss Abel did not remember the men complaining when they picked up their pay since there was not much other work to be had. "All the workers, had running water and electricity in their houses and everyone was proud of that," Miss Abel told me.

Often "The Company" as employees often called it, built housing for the workers and charged about $10 a month rent. The company houses were sometimes painted one color, such as dark red or green. The identical two or three-room wooden structures stood row upon row near the mills. Like the military today, mill workers had a commissary of sorts where they could buy groceries, dry goods and other supplies. Often lumber mills would pay their employees in credit at these stores, rather than in cash. The mill employees complained about that.

In a small town, you may not personally know every person in town, but you know "of" them. That's how another Bagdadian, Anise Presley Smith, remembers the Pittmans. "I was too young to know them. Jackie was a good bit older than I was, but I do remember them being 'Bagdadians," she said. "They lived in town for a time ... it was a two-story house they lived in, down a block or so from my family's."

My family understood the hard economic times were common not only to the mill communities in the South, but to the entire country, affected as it was by the Great Depression. Even then, at about 12 or 13, Bessie despised the poverty she saw herself as living in. In her second autobiography Aunt Jackie remembers those times as being the most difficult in her life.

Jackie

"I hear a lot about poverty in the United States at the present time. Sometimes it gives me a laugh but usually it makes me mad. The gray clad boys from the advertising row on Madison Avenue and the politicians who make a profession of talking about poverty where it does not exist so that they can get credit for caring for it, just don't know what poverty is. I do. I lived with it for the first eight or ten years of my life. If you don't where your next meal is coming from or the meal after that and you have no bed to sleep on and are happy to have the bare floor for a mattress, and if your clothes are made out of used floursacks, you can be sure you are poverty-stricken."

There are still a few old people in Bagdad who lived in the mill era who remember the Pittman men who worked beside them.

"My brother worked with the Pittmans," said Rubin Smith, now 90, a Bagdad resident told me. "I worked at the mill too," he said, holding up a hand missing two fingers as his proof.

"It was dangerous working in the mills ... There were a lot of accidents—men working in the forests with crosscuts saws, or a boiler would blow up, or a belt on the saws would break, or somebody would get caught in the machinery," he said.

Though many of the Bagdadians, who would have known the Pittmans, are dead now, my Aunt Bessie Pittman is still remembered. When they talk about her today, they refer to her as "Jackie", the name she chose for herself as a young adult when she lived on her own in New York City. In *We Remember Bagdad*, the area's architectural history, the names 'Jacqueline Cochran' and 'Bessie Pittman' are indexed in the back of the book and cross-reference each other. The short entry highlights her accomplishments and tells that Aunt Jackie lived in Bagdad. Without explanation, the copy under the entry Bessie Pittman states, "She changed her name to Jacqueline Cochran".

Bessie and her sisters started school at the two-story Bagdad schoolhouse on Simpson Street.

Grandmother finished high school in her hometown in Milton, Florida and for a time taught school. She taught wherever she was needed until she became a mother. Then she devoted her time to taking care of her family only substitute teaching occasionally. She sent Henry, Myrtle and Mamie to Bagdad Elementary and tried to send Bessie, but Bessie didn't take too well to school. First grade was a nightmare for Bessie but at least it was short-lived. The way Bessie tells it, the teacher, Anna Thompson, whose name shows up in the old Bagdad school records, took a ruler to Bessie's hand on the third day of Bessie's first school year. Bessie hit her back and ran out of the schoolhouse, never to return, at least for the rest of that school year.

Grandmother tried to get around Bessie's rebelliousness by escorting her personally to the schoolhouse each morning. But by the time Grandmother would make it back to the house, Bessie would be there. Bessie was headstrong like Grandmother. Bessie got her way ... almost. Grandmother finally gave up on making Bessie go to school, but she still made her learn her ABCs at home.

Bessie did go back to school the next year and because she liked the new teacher, Miss Bostwick, this time she stayed. She even enthusiastically agreed to an after-school job carrying firewood for ten cents a week to the second-story apartment where Miss Bostwick lived. Bessie fell in love with the beautiful, cozy apartment, the teacher's fashionable clothing and the extra attention she received from the woman with the exotic northern accent. When Miss Bostwick left Bagdad to return North after a year of teaching in Bagdad, Bessie was heartbroken. And that was the end of her formal education. She referred to herself as a second-grade drop out but she made it a long way on her brief education. As an adult she addressed the graduating students at Harvard Business School, was a trustee at George Washington University and held four honorary Doctor's degrees. Despite her own difficulties with education, Aunt Jackie believed strongly in the importance of having one. I know she personally helped pay for schooling for several family members and for a number of people she barely knew.

Aunt Jackie's self-confidence remained resolute throughout her life. Jackie was smart and well aware of the gender role differences, but she made her own rules. She didn't forget much either, particularly if she felt there was some injustice done to her.

The doll was such a case. At the end of her life, along with her huge collections of trophies, plaques, medals and other awards, she had a doll collection. In that collection was a doll she had when she was a little girl. It was very important to her. She said she won it in a lottery and Grandmother took it away from her to give to Mamie's young daughter, Willie Mae. Now grown, Norma—Willie Mae's youngest daughter—said her mother told her Grandmother actually won this beautiful fancy doll in a mill commissary store 'drawing', and that she did take it away from Jackie—for reasons unknown—and give it to

SUPERWOMAN Jacqueline Cochran

Willie Mae. Norma said it was actually my grandfather who told Grandmother to give Willie Mae the doll. There's no telling what really happened, but Jackie never forgot this 'grave' injustice. Twenty years later when Jackie was doing well for herself in New York City, she invited Willie Mae and her daughter Mildred, who was just a toddler to come live with her. There was only one condition. Willie Mae had to give Jackie back the doll she had lost decades before. Jackie got the doll and she did help Willie Mae. She let her live with her for a while then set her up in her own small apartment. She paid for Willie Mae to attend a business school, and when she graduated Jackie gave her a job helping her to manage her personal business. She sent Willie Mae out to California to live and set her up in an office in Jackie's beauty salon in the fashionable Ambassador Hotel. Willie Mae was an attractive woman and favored Jackie. Her daughter, Mildred, does too. Willie Mae died, at the age of 46, in 1959 of cancer. Jackie's sister, Mamie died of breast cancer and several other members in Mamie's immediate family died of cancer as well. One of Mamie's sons, Lloyd, died in a motorcycle accident. Jerry, Aunt Mamie's youngest child, is the only one of her children living. He is still in California.

Bessie was partial to dolls, but she was still a tomboy. I never cared that much for dolls when I was a little girl. Paper dolls were okay I guess. Later I loved real babies, particularly my own dear daughters, Linda and Vicki. But there was one doll I will never forget. When I was about 10 years old, Jackie sent me a doll from France. Unfortunately I lost it. Aunt Jackie was always sending us things. This time it was a doll made of felt. I had never seen anything like it. I distinctly remember it had real hair and was dressed in an aqua coat and hat.

Although a dozen years separated their births, my father and Bessie were like 'peas in a pod,' personality-wise. That's probably what made it hard for them to get along later. They were both headstrong. Once, either one made a decision he, or she, was right, that was it. There was no giving in, no going back.

On returning home from his travels as a sailor, my father met my mother, Ethel Mae Ingram in 1915. When he met Ethel in Millville, Fla. where she was visiting her aunt and uncle, he knew immediately he wanted to settle down with her as his wife. She thought it a fine plan too and only two weeks later, just before Christmas, Daddy asked for her hand in marriage. The quickness shocked her parents. Ethel was an obedient daughter who had played the organ for her church. She had done well in school and loved to read. There were no objections, however and they were married. The marriage lasted 55 years until my mother died in 1970.

Ethel fit in beautifully with the rest of the Pittman family who were also living in Millville. Born and raised in Pansey, Alabama, Mother too, came from a large family. She was quiet, firm and hardworking. My father was smart and snappy, but Mother was the wise one, patient, the peacemaker. I am most like her in wanting to avoid conflict. I don't think negativity is necessary. Mother felt that way too and did not allow arguments. I guess I take after her in that way.

After World War I started, my parents moved to Florence, Alabama where my brother, Joseph Edward, Jr. was born. Dad worked on a war project building the Muscle Shoals Dam. Grandfather, Grandmother, Bessie and the rest of the family, except Myrtle, stayed in

Millville. Myrtle had married W.R. Alford and she stayed behind to give birth to the first of eight children they were to have during their marriage.

Daddy was not the only one who fell in love with Ethel. At nine years old, Bessie did too. Whereas Mollie, Bessie's mother, my Grandmother was demanding, at times strident, with an explosive temper, Ethel was unflappable, had a calm voice and was always ready to help Bessie in any way. Mother was an excellent seamstress but quite modest about it. I can hardly believe it, but Mother told me she allowed Jackie to enter some of her fancywork in Jackie's name in the Chicago World's Fair and even won a ribbon. When Jackie was starting up her new business in New York, she would send the business letters she wrote, for Mother to look over for grammar and spelling errors. Throughout her life, Jackie lacked confidence in this area, but she was smart to get help with it. Mother loved Jackie dearly and did everything she could to help her.

Chapter Three: The Unknown from Noma

The Pittmans moved at least once a year to follow the millwork. The family was close. Even though Daddy, Uncle Henry and the aunts began their own families, often all of these families moved together. In 1920 Aunt Mamie and her new family were living in the small farming community of Knox Hill, just outside Ponce De Leon, Florida. The rest of the family lived about 30 miles away in the small community of Amarillo, now nonexistent, outside of Paxton. Paxton was a new town, only about six years old, the product of a new sawmill. There was also a planing mill, a dry kiln, three drying sheds, an office, commissary, post office, a hotel and four rows of company houses, all built on Paxton Hill.

Grandmother was a good cook and a queen bee organizer. She ran several boardinghouses during her lifetime. We know she later ran one in downtown Pensacola on Alcaniz Street. She was operating one in Paxton when my sister Gwendolyn was born. Grandmother was small in stature but, she could get things done. When she spoke, people listened and obeyed. Not everyone liked Grandmother, but I adored her. She was the opposite of my grandfather. He was tall, thin and quiet: she was short, sort of plump and vocal. She was entertaining, like my father, and she spent a lot of time with me...teaching me to embroider and just talking about family and things. In later years she lived with my mother and daddy and she told me many family stories. She told me how Bessie—like her other daughters—married early, as was the custom. Her stories, as well as stories Mother and Daddy told me, provided the framework for my research about Jackie in recent years.

Bessie was 14 years old and Robert Cochran was ten years older when they were married at the Early County courthouse in Blakely, Georgia on November 13, 1920. Blakely was only a couple of hours away from Paxton, north to Dothan, Alabama then east across the state line into the State of Georgia. Like in many small southern towns even today, the courthouse was the hub of Blakely. The licensed Ordinary C.C. Law who married them more than likely did not know Bessie's real age or he could not have legally joined them together because 18 was the minimum age to wed. As in many small Southern towns today, anyone younger than that must have their parents' written permission.

We are not sure how Aunt Bessie and Robert met, but Robert was a machinist by trade and his family was from Noma, another small town, more of a community than a town, about 35 miles east of Paxton. Lutrell Hinote, a Noma native who later moved to nearby DeFuniak Springs, said she thought the couple met while Robert attended the Thomas Industrial Institute in DeFuniak Springs. Our family later lived in what was referred to as the 'TII Building' on Second Avenue after the industrial school closed down in 1924. More than seventy years later, renters can still find rooms available in what is now called the Chautauqua Apartments. I was a small child when we lived there and I only remember my brother I.D. rocking in a rocking chair there. He had a crippled foot. He would sit there and rock so long; he actually wore grooves in the floor.

Mrs. Hinote remembers, "Robert Cochran and I had gone to school together," she said. "I remember when they

(Robert and Bessie) got married, because he brought his new bride back here [to Noma] ... After the wedding they came back and lived a short time in a big white two-story house with his parents. I can still see that two-story so easily in my mind. Later they moved into Bonifay, some 14 miles south, where more of the young people were living at the time ... I read about her later when she became famous because we all knew who she was—Jacqueline Cochran. I remember thinking how what she told the newspapers wasn't quite true. I saw Bob at a school reunion in the 1970s. We talked about the good old times, but not about Bessie."

Noma is a quiet place to live, only two miles east of Esto, another quiet place to live and only 11 miles north of Bonifay—the county seat of Holmes County. Even neighbors who live less than an hour away do not know where Noma is. Just before one arrives in Noma on State Road 2, there are oddly, not one, but two state Department of Transportation signs identifying the community. Noma's two churches, a Baptist and an Assembly of God, share a cemetery. Because the town is so small, it almost comes as a surprise that a city hall exists, housed in a large metal building. It closes by noon on weekdays. Next door to the city hall are a library and a tiny trailer filled with books. When the Alabama-Florida Lumber Mill closed in 1921, blowing its mill whistle 23 times to mark closing day, many area businesses closed too. A general exodus followed with the population of about 1,500 dwindling to the estimated 220 residents of today. Most Noma residents travel to the nearby towns of Graceville, Dothan, or Bonifay to work. Other than an abandoned old wooden house here or there, there is little evidence of the busy mill town that once boasted two general stores, a post office, two hotels, a blacksmith, millinery, drug store, cotton gin and a livery.

Four months after marrying Robert, Bessie gave birth to Robert Cochran Jr. in Pensacola, Florida. It wasn't long after that the new family moved far from family, more than 500 miles away, to the other end of the state—Miami.

My parents and grandparents had already moved a few miles farther south to work in a mill in the Lakewood community. Lakewood today claims to be the highest point in Florida—345 feet above sea level. Although former Congressman Bob Sikes tried to dub it "Florida's Mountain," that name never caught on, maybe because the elevation is little more than a plateau 900 feet by 400 feet. The scenery is pretty, if you like to look at pine trees.

It was in Lakewood, in 1922, my brother, Ira DeWitt, was born to my parents. We called him I.D. In the next year or so the Lakewood mill owned by Britton Timber Co. burned. Fires were common occurrences at mills in those days. That particular mill burned three times.

Then the Pittmans moved 20 miles south to DeFuniak Springs, where my grandfather, my dad and Uncle Henry took jobs working with the large W. B. Harbeson Lumber Mill. My grandfather was a millwright there, meaning he was in charge of keeping the mill's machinery in working order. Daddy ran a logging train that went into the forests and returned with carloads of felled trees. He also worked as a carpenter and painter. He was active from 1931 to 1935 in DeFuniak Springs Wildey Lodge #14 of the International Order of Odd Fellows, a civic organization. He worked for the U.S. Government during WWII as an engineer of sorts, building airfields. I've always wondered if Aunt Jackie ever landed a plane on any airfield he had helped build. Towards the end of his life he ran a grocery and market. He liked variety in his work, which must have been hard on my mother, but she never complained. Lucy Marse, who lived in Freeport, Florida until she recently passed away, said her brother worked with my father, both in the mill and on carpentry projects. "It was just before the Depression and times were hard for everyone. There were days when people would go hungry and there were plenty of children of the mill workers who, if they did have shoes, had raggedy ones," said Marsh.

During these difficult times Daddy would bring homeless people to our home to share our meals. He never passed a hitchhiker by without offering him a ride, and a meal if he needed one. Now I know it set an example of love for us, but then I just thought that was what everyone did.

The DeFuniak Springs mill was one of the largest of the many mills owned by Harbeson. He was one of the South's leading lumber manufacturers and he owned great tracts of lands and dozens of mills throughout Mississippi, Georgia and Florida. He made his family's home in DeFuniak Springs. He also owned many hotels in Florida, the largest being the once-famous, now-demolished, 500-room San Carlos Hotel in Pensacola.

It did not take but a few years of marriage for a problem to surface between Robert and Bessie. Her name was Ethel May Mathis, and when Bessie learned of the affair she moved home to DeFuniak Springs, bringing four-year-old Robert, Jr. with her.

When Bessie went down to the Walton County Courthouse to file divorce papers, Grandmother went with her. Grandmother testified before Judge A. G. Campbell, "Bessie was, 'my daughter, baby child ... Yes, I've visited the couple once or twice since they had been married, once a few months after the baby was born."

Aunt Bessie had this to say under oath about her soon-to-be-ex-husband:

Q. Where were you living when you separated?
A. In Miami.
Q. Did you leave him?
A. I did.
Q. Have you been living here ever since?
A. Yes, sir.
Q. Have you relatives here?
A. All my people are here.
Q. What was your maiden name?
A. Bessie Pittman.
Q. Was this Matthew woman a relative?
A. No, sir.
Q. You say you have every reason to believe that your husband and this woman were guilty of adultery. Have you given all the reasons why you believe it?
A. Yes, sir.
Q. After you had satisfied yourself that your husband was guilty of adultery, did you live with your husband and if so, how long after?
A. We separated right then after it became a provable fact.

In DeFuniak Springs my older sister, Bennie Rae was born in the spring of 1925. I came along the next year in December. Three years later, my baby brother Gordon was born.

During the years she lived in DeFuniak Springs, Aunt Bessie moved around within the town. Sometimes she lived alone with her baby; sometimes she stayed with her parents. She and Robert Jr. also lived for months with my family.

I remember living on Second Street, Plateau Avenue and on Highway 90 during our DeFuniak Spring years. Mamie and Myrtle had both married DeFuniak men and were busy raising families. So by now, all the Pittmans were together again.

As a young mother whose husband was never around, Aunt Bessie must have appeared out of the norm to DeFuniak society. Her stylish appearance and liberal manner probably didn't ease the minds of the conservative church-going population. She was a 'looker', a term old timers used to describe a woman with a striking appearance. At 5'7" and 120 pounds, she must have been seen as a strikingly beautiful woman walking along the main street downtown. She had a pretty face, but it was her large, dark brown eyes that drew and held attention. She knew which of the latest fashions flattered her perfect figure. My mother, who was a talented seamstress, made some of her dresses. Mother also made all of our school clothes and we considered ourselves the best-dressed kids in school.

There was a lot more to Aunt Bessie than her shapely figure and pretty face. I think DeFuniak Springs did not know quite what to do with her. She would go to church with our family and later would be seen smoking a cigarette on the porch behind Will Meig's Mill store. In the 1920s, smoking may have been winked at in a larger, more cosmopolitan town, but DeFuniak saw it as a symbol of rebelliousness. The Pittmans were known to be decent, hardworking people, yet Jackie had her own ideas of how to live life. In later years I talked enough with DeFuniak

SUPERWOMAN Jacqueline Cochran

folks who knew her as a young woman. Jackie had quite a reputation for being on the wild side. She was pretty and smart and she knew it. Today, no one would probably think much about it, but then it caused a stir in the small town where everyone knew everyone else's business.

Whether you liked her or not, you did not forget Bessie. Seventy years later, legends, myths and gossip about Aunt Bessie still circulate in DeFuniak Springs and the surrounding areas. Many know her by both names: Bessie Pittman and Jackie Cochran. Memories and opinions of some of the old timers who knew her—many of which are quite elderly—differ by 180 degrees. Several of DeFuniak's elderly women, demurred from talking about Bessie Pittman, saying they didn't want to take part in any negative gossip. And there are still old men around whose eyes still light up when they remember Bessie. Who's to say who's memory is accurate, but they remembered her as "kind", "wild", "smart as a whip", and "beautiful".

"Yes, I remember her, but when I first saw her she was a Cochran," said Mrs. Weba Paul, who worked as a court reporter in Walton County for 30 years and also worked as secretary to Commanding General Grandison Gardner at Eglin Air Force Base nearby. "I never did see a husband, but she had a boy with her, a beautiful child. I was big enough then to overhear the women talk about how awful she was to hang out by the mill store, which belonged to Will Meigs.

"... Behind my friend, Kate Dawkins', house there was a place where they kept the mules for the mill. They called it 'the lot'. We would climb on that high fence and sit there just so we could watch her smoke a cigarette on Meig's Store porch. She was the first woman we'd ever seen smoke. Our mothers certainly would not have allowed it if they had known what we were doing." Another resident, Lucy Marse, did know Bessie but said she, "didn't want to talk about the negatives of Bessie."

"Her family went regular to church," said Marse. "Seems like Mr. Pittman didn't go regular and Bessie didn't go every Sunday. Some of them would go to a little Methodist Church in West End (the west end of town). It's still there. We went there, too. After the service we would all leave there and go to my Aunt Minnie's Holiness Church. Aunt Minnie was the preacher there. It was nearby and those services were hours long and would still be going on when the Methodist Church let out."

The reason Mrs. Marse did not see my grandfather might have been because he was a member at the First Baptist Church, joining in 1925. My father, mother, brothers, sisters and I also attended the First Baptist Church. Though Mother read her Bible a lot and was very strong in her belief of God, she often stayed home to prepare the huge Sunday meal. Those big family meals are among my best memories. I still dream of them, all of us sitting around a big table Mother would have loaded down with bowls of vegetables like greens, creamed corn, butterbeans, peas, fried okra, accompanied by a big platter of fried chicken or maybe fish. Dad didn't eat pork and Mother would not eat beef, therefore we often had both so as to satisfy everyone. Mother did not believe in our eating too many sweets, so she made after school treats such as gingerbread and saved her lane cakes and nut cakes for special occasions and holidays. Her biscuits were the best.

Today people living in the south end of Walton County, directly on the Gulf Coast, claim the small town of DeFuniak Springs, which is the county seat in the north end is at least a decade, if not two, behind the times. The south

SUPERWOMAN Jacqueline Cochran

end is growing so fast, and changing so rapidly with the continual construction of new restaurants, condos and other businesses, it's easy to get lost even if you once knew your way around. Being 'behind', doesn't bother most of the town's residents. They see it as more of a compliment than a put-down. Even 68 years after Bessie left, DeFuniak Springs is still very much a traditional, family-oriented, conservative community. The town has enough churches so that if the entire population of about 10,000 were churchgoers, the average congregation would be less than 200. The divorces are posted in *The DeFuniak Herald*—a weekly, published continuously since 1888—along with the marriages, obituaries, building permits and city police and county sheriff arrest reports. A yearly subscription was $1 when it started and its owner, Larklin Cleveland ran a slogan "Liked by many, cussed by some, read by everybody." News travels faster by word of mouth in a small town than any press ink could flow, still many subscribe to *The Herald* so they can compare the black and white 'facts' with what they find out for themselves. The townspeople of DeFuniak treasure their tranquility and aren't in much of a hurry to catch up with the south end. The town is quieter now than in the late 1800s when the lumber mills were thriving and DeFuniak Springs was considered the cultural center for the area between Pensacola and Tallahassee.

Anna Reardon wrote several columns about Bessie, among the hundreds she wrote over the years for *The DeFuniak Herald-Breeze*. They were published years after Bessie changed her name to Jackie. Reardon recalled Bessie lived in the west end of town known as the Harbeson Mill Quarters in the 1930s. Reardon's columns express pride in the "local girl's" accomplishments, talked about her closeness to her family but openly questioned why Jackie never acknowledged DeFuniak Springs and why the media never questioned Jackie about her orphan story.

Laura Wilkerson, 83, remembers being neighbors with the Pittmans.

"They (the Pittmans) lived up the road from us.... Bessie had a boyfriend and he had a grocery store," she said.

Like many of the area residents still do daily, Bessie and her friends more than likely strolled around spring-fed Lake DeFuniak (hence the name DeFuniak Springs). Locals have always boasted of it being almost perfectly round, second in circularity only to a lake somewhere in Russia. It takes slow walkers about 15 minutes to make it around the mile of sidewalk just beyond the lake's edges. Several hundred feet farther up the grassy slopes, another sidewalk encircles "the lake yard," as it is referred to. Sometimes the sidewalk runs along the outer perimeter of the concrete street, called "Circle Drive"; sometimes it switches to the inside of the street. House-high camellias are scattered throughout the lake yard, along with old magnolias, live oaks, dogwoods and even a few of the area's remaining longleaf pines.

As children, we loved the weekly ritual of walking with our parents to the lake yard to play on Saturday afternoons. Father would give us small bags of little red-hot candies to eat. During the summer months, it was one of my greatest pleasures to walk with Mother and my sisters and brothers to the lake for a swim.

Like petals on a sunflower, large two-story ante-bellum homes sit on the perimeter of the lake yard. One of only three buildings within the lake yard, The DeFuniak Springs

Library was one of my favorite places to go when we lived in town. Built in 1886, it is the state's oldest library that has stayed open continuously in the same place. Dwarfed by a large oak, the quaint Victorian style library with its dark roof and white scalloped wood shingles on its front is everything a library should be. Stepping inside, you instantly become aware of quiet because no matter what shoes you're wearing, they make noise when you walk on the polished hard wood floors. So you start trying to be quiet. In strong contrast to the charming outward appearance and the inherent inner silence, today wicked-looking weapons of war from medieval times fill the library walls. Donated by one of the founders of the town, Kenneth Bruce, the collection of medieval weaponry makes the library into a museum as well. Curvy-edged swords longer than a horse, hang beside daggers, axes, spiked balls, heavy helmets and a chain-mesh shirt which perhaps did, or didn't, save some knight's life. How odd it is to see these ancient weapons of war on the walls of such a peaceful place. Mother took us during the summer to the regular 'story times' the library held for children. I loved curling up with the book in the reading room in the back of the library. There were—and still are—large glass windows all around and it overlooks the lake. Reading was encouraged in our family. In our home in Marianna, in 1936, Dad built us our own special reading room, which was really the roof above our house. He made special steps for us up the oak trees on one side of the porch so we could step off onto the roof and have our own special place.

The other two buildings in the lake yard are the Presbyterian Church built in 1883 and the Chautauqua building. When the family moved to DeFuniak Springs, the Florida Chautauqua was in its prime, attracting thousands of visitors, who came by horse, on foot and by train. William Jennings Bryan called the 100 Chautauquas scattered throughout American, "the people's university" although they were originally created as an educational program for Sunday school teachers. Held during the cool spring months, it was considered the winter home for the cultural, education and religious activities of the popular Chautauqua Festival held in New York each summer. The month long series of events, lectures, workshops, plus entertainment associated with the Chautauqua fell apart under the pressure of the Great Depression, but was revived many years later and is active today, drawing nationally known speakers and hundreds of attendees.

The town of DeFuniak is immediately north of the lake yard and has one main street. A train depot built in 1882 by the Pennsylvania and Atlantic Railroad Company, which later became Louisville and Nashville, sits by the tracks between town and the lake yard. Several years ago it received a successful face-lift. A bright red caboose is permanently parked nearby. Downtown merchants have painted their old brick buildings, added awnings, planters, and hold several festivals with firework displays over the lake to remind area residents there is more to the world than shopping at the Super Wal-Mart a couple of miles south of town. In the past the town's wealthier women, and somehow Bessie too, bought stylish dresses and delicate lingerie from the upscale W.E. Parish & Company, owned and operated by Miss Anna and Miss Jennie Parish. Those who could afford it came from many miles around to shop at Parrish' which also had its own milliner to create custom hats for the ladies.

Two blocks west on the main street, sat Beach & Rogers Mill, a much smaller mill than Harbeson's, its neighbor on the right. Today, members of the local rural electric cooperative pay bills in the same redbrick office where Harbeson's employees picked up their paychecks a century ago. Opposite the office's entrance and across the railroad tracks, sat a business owned by Will Meigs. He lived a block away in a large house with his wife, Ella, and their family on Live Oak Avenue. Across from them lived one of Florida's most colorful governors, Sidney J. Catts, who moved to DeFuniak when his term ended in 1921.

In Meigs' white building, the first floor was a grocery store. The upstairs rooms of Meigs' Store, as it was called, were rented out to boarders. I've been told my Aunt Bessie was one. Downstairs—groceries, dry goods and shoes, clothes and other necessities of life lined the store's walls. They were sold to mill workers and their families through a credit system set up with the mill. Just one block from the Meigs' store lot Howard Nowling still lives in the house where he has lived for 85 years. His parents moved there when he was 2 years old.

"Pretty much everyone knew Bessie and Meigs had a thing for each other," said Nowling. "She always dressed real nice and got her clothes from Parrish store downtown. That was a real nice store. Expensive.

"She was a beautiful woman and a lovely person too," he said. "I was crazy about her, even if I was only 15 and she was about 20. I was her 'runabout'. She didn't drive and I would drive her downtown to shop. Later, she bought a brand new Ford convertible. Actually 'someone' bought it for her. It had a rumble seat and she would let me borrow it when I needed it for a date ... I was going to school at that time and working for Will Meigs, the store owner."

Nowling and our family members aren't the only ones to remember Jackie's little red roadster. Many DeFuniak residents remember it, too. Hank Douglass said his father, Angus Gillis Douglass was thrilled when he came home from his Ford dealership one day and told his family about how a young woman came in, paid $700 cash for a car and drove off with it. Paying cash was unheard of then in that place. "Dad was practically in shock he was so excited. No one had ever done that before," said Douglass.

Other neighbors remember Bessie living above Will Meigs' store. Mrs. Maude Mayo lives two houses down from the now-empty lot. She was about nine or ten years old when she lived a few blocks away from where she lives now. She remembers shopping regularly with her parents at Meigs' store and on one occasion seeing Bessie.

"She was standing in her robe leaning against the railing out on the second floor balcony. I knew who she was because people talked about her and I knew she later became famous as a flier. Seems like she lived alone then," said Mrs. Mayo.

There are many DeFuniak Springs townspeople like Mayo and Nowling who have lived many decades in one place. Fewer moves and fewer faces may be why such townspeople can remember their next-door neighbors so well so many years later.

Cecil "Wendy" Neel has lived his 76 years in the same house on Douglass Avenue he was born in. Both he and his sister, Sybil, stayed on in the house after their parents died. The Pittmans were once their next-door neighbors, before I was born.

"Bessie wasn't a girl when she lived next door; she was a young woman," Neel recalls. "I used to walk to school with I.D. Pittman. He was about my age."

"Everybody was poor then, except we didn't know it. Like most of the families around here they had a garden behind their house and a few animals: a cow, pigs and a couple of chickens. Seems like Bessie was just in and out—visiting—it was not like she lived there all the time. She was considerable older than me, so I didn't know her too well," he said.

Neel said many families have lived in the small house next door since the Pittmans. "The Pittmans used to keep it neat," said Neel. Now the house appears abandoned even if a large family does indeed live there. Car tires, scattered rusted toys and garbage in the yard have made the place an eyesore in the modest neighborhood.

The storeowner William Franklin Meigs was a leader in the community. He came from a family of active community leaders. His father, Charlie Meigs, was Walton County commissioner and other family members were in the U.S. Senate and on the Supreme Court. Will's wife, Ella, was always sick, though no one recalls with exactly what.

"Well... my mother used to say someone had pulled her corset too tight, which was a common way of saying she was probably something of a hypochondriac," said Elizabeth Neel, a niece of Will Meigs. "Still she was never too sick to go on a trip somewhere," joked Mrs. Neel, who lives in a white two-story Victorian home on the lake yard. She said the family knew of the affair between Bessie and Will but did not discuss it. "My mother intimated once, there was something between them, but that was all I ever heard. I was young. Those things just weren't discussed," she said.

Even though I was quite young I remember family talk of Will Meigs and Aunt Bessie. We knew that he bought her a little red roadster.

Will's grandson, Bill, an attorney, living in the nearby town of Niceville, chuckles when asked about the affair. "Yes, we know about Bessie. We called her 'Bess'. Grandpa was a sport. He was very keen on Bess."

Jackie wrote she never had a child, but it may be that the memory of losing her 4-year-old son in a house fire was so awful she forced herself to forget, or never wanted anyone to remind her of it. The child's name was Robert Cochran Jr., according to his birth certificate, which named Robert Cochran Sr. as the father, and Bessie Cochran as the mother.

Billie Pittman Ayers and Beth Dees

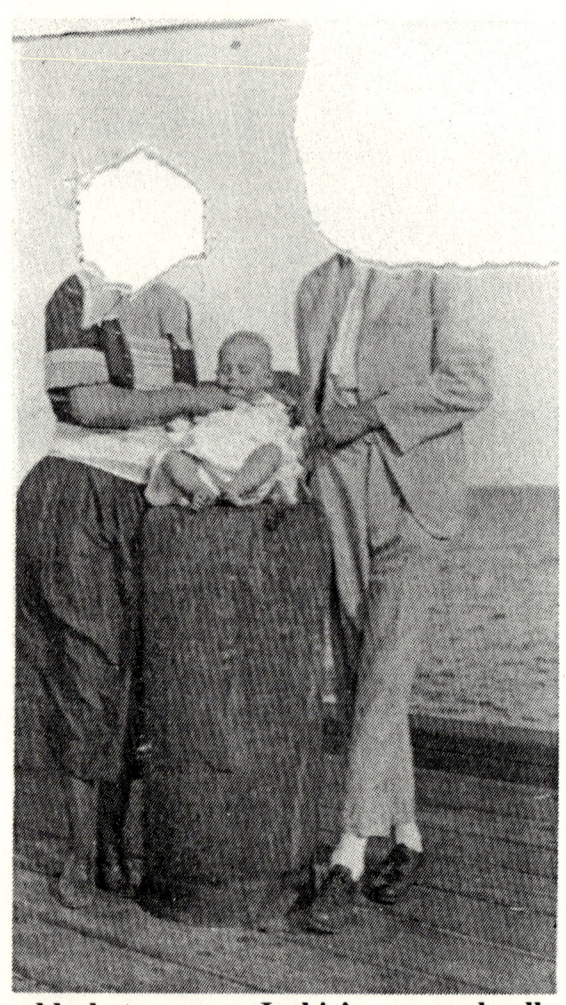

In this odd photo among Jackie's personal collection in the Dwight D. Eisenhower Library family members believe the child to be Robert Jr. and the defaced people to be his grandmother and grandfather, possibly standing dockside in Pensacola, the city of the child's birth.

Chapter Four: The Phoenix Flies

When my sister, Gwendolyn was five years old, she remembers seeing Aunt Bessie bending over the dead body of her only son—Robert Jr. The little boy with blonde curly hair and a pleasant disposition had been burned severely in a fire that started in the yard. The article about it in DeFuniak Spring's weekly newspaper *The Breeze,* read,

"One of the saddest accidents, culminating in the death of the victim, was that which overtook little Robert H. Corcoran (sic) Jr. Friday the 29th. The little fellow, not quite five years old, at an early hour of the morning, while alone in the back yard, set fire to some paper, with a match he had found. This in turn, set fire to his clothes, and in a moment he was enveloped in flames.

"The first to notice his predicament was Mr. James Bell, a very near neighbor, who rushed to his aid, pulling the burning clothes from the child, himself receiving bad burns on his hands.

"The mother, grandfather and grandmother were immediately on the scene, physicians sent for and everything possible done to relieve the little sufferer. From the first, it was perceived that his life could not possibly be saved and all efforts were directed toward relieving him of pain for the few hours remaining of his earthly life. This was done and the dear little boy was soon at ease. He regained consciousness up to an hour before his demise, talking to friends and relatives and explaining how the tragedy occurred.

"Robert H. Corcoran, Jr. was the only child of Robert H. Corcoran and his wife, Bessie Lee (Pittman) Corcoran.

With his mother, he resided with his grandparents, Pittman, at the end of town."

He was buried two days later beneath a small heart-shaped headstone in the Magnolia Cemetery just east of town. Today it is black with age and barely readable. This ordeal surrounds Gwen's first memory of her aunt, and it is her only memory of Robert Jr., who had been a playmate and was her age.

Gwen told me, "I just remember her sitting on his bed ...and I was standing beside her. I don't remember other people being there, or the funeral later, or even Aunt Bessie crying, though I imagine she did. It's like a photograph in my mind."

Bessie did nothing as depression settled in. She stayed with her parents and also continued with living with my family off and on. Bessie would rarely speak of her child again. She kept some of his things in a trunk for years. Later in life she wrote she never had children. It was as if Robert Jr. had never been born. Maybe in her mind he never had. Maybe that was the only way she knew how to survive the tragedy.

A year and a half later after the child's death, Bessie filed for divorce from Robert Cochran at the Walton County Courthouse. Documents could not be found in the Walton County courthouse finalizing the divorce. Bessie kept her married name of Cochran.

Bessie had too many hard memories of DeFuniak Springs: the divorce and Robert Junior's death among them. Maybe it was the sum of these reasons that made the 20-year-old decide to leave. She traveled 100 miles west to Mobile, Alabama to start fresh. Though she left us behind, she moved in with other family, her mother's sister—

SUPERWOMAN Jacqueline Cochran

Amanda Grant-Smith, her husband and her cousin—Allie Frank Laws.

To help Bessie her get her mind off her problems her Aunt Amanda, Grandmother's sister, sent her to The Eloise McAndrews Beauty Parlor on St. Joseph's Street to receive training as a beautician. Soon Bessie was working in a beauty shop located in the Battle House Hotel on Royale Street downtown. Another cousin, Hubert Grant, known as "Pinkie", knew Bessie was severely depressed and was very attentive to her. He was working at that time for Radio Station WODX, providing sports news commentary. He would stop by each day to talk with Jackie. The close family ties and Pinkie's special attention helped see Jackie through the worst of times. She and Pinkie remained close. He went on to work for Radio Station WABB and later had a television program on station WALA.

In Jackie's early years of flying, Pinkie interviewed her with Wiley Post, a pioneer pilot and the first man to fly solo around the world. Post helped prove high altitude flight was possible. He lost his life in 1935 in an air crash with Will Rogers in Alaska. Both were friends of Jackie's.

Bessie came home in 1928 when my grandfather died suddenly of a stroke. All the family gathered. I was young but I remember he paid us a lot of attention, unlike most adults. He was buried in the Pittman family plot in Magnolia Cemetery near Robert Cochran, Jr.

My sister Gwen, who was older, remembered him well. "Grandpa was laid out on the bed and Daddy was shaving him. Seems like I had been taken away (by an adult) from the house earlier and that was what I saw when I came back. There were gardenias in the room. Since that day I have not been able to stand the smell of gardenias. I remember him as one of the most loving, gentle people I have ever known. He was a railroad man in later years and had a big railroad watch and when I was a little girl he would hold it up to my ear and let me listen to its tick. It had a very loud tick and he would tell me there was a little boy inside it chopping wood. Of course I believed him."

Bessie went back to work in a beauty parlor in Pensacola located in the Blount building on the corner of Palafox and Garden streets, across from the famous San Carlos Hotel. Harbeson, the mill owner from DeFuniak Springs bought the San Carlos in 1922, twelve years after it was built. Eight stories high, finished with pearl-gray stucco and multitudinous stone carved trimmings, the San Carlos was the center of the city's social life and considered one of the finest hotels in the South. Sadly, the historic landmark deteriorated and was demolished in 1993.

Now deceased, Phil Harris was a beau of Bessie's when she lived in DeFuniak Springs. Over a half a century later, he confessed he drove the 160 miles round trip from home to Pensacola just to see her now and then. Getting a manicure gave him the excuse he needed.

"I was running a grocery store business in DeFuniak Springs and I used to go over to Pensacola to drop in and get a manicure from her. I would pay her $5, but it really didn't cost that much. I had a good paying job so I would give her a big tip," Harris said.

Bessie went at life full tilt while living in the port city of Pensacola. Taking lessons from a Texas state-dancing champion, she put her toe-tapping knowledge to good use at dances at the U.S. Naval Aeronautics Station, which was, renamed the Pensacola Naval Air Station in 1917. In 1914, because of its year-round flying weather, Pensacola was the Navy's choice to base its aviation unit. By 1917, the base boasted 38 aviators among its personnel of about 500 men.

SUPERWOMAN Jacqueline Cochran

I think—based on other family member's memories—her dating the Pensacola airmen may have benefited Bessie in more ways than fun. She may have been able to win an important bet later about her learning to fly so quickly because she already had some knowledge of airplanes. Even though I know the military isn't supposed to let civilians on the planes, it wouldn't surprise me a bit if Bessie didn't talk one of her airmen friends into taking her out and teaching her a little about airplanes. She was a charmer and a daredevil.

Bessie was flipping through a beauty trade magazine one day and spotted an ad that motivated her. The ad touted advanced training classes for beauty operators who wanted to learn to do the new "doos". Bessie was always looking for ways of improving herself so she moved to Philadelphia to start classes and so impressed the school's director Bessie became a teacher instead of a student. After only nine months she became disillusioned with the school. She thought it unfair and unethical the school accepted money from people Bessie felt unlikely candidates to be beauty operators. She left, and headed home to Pensacola. Bessie quickly grew restless, missing the excitement and bright lights of the big city. She headed north again, this time for the brightest lights in America—New York City.

While she was up North, her brother Henry, who was a member of the Merchant Marine, died. He drowned, along with four other crewmembers, when their barge—The Northern Light—loaded with phosphate rock and headed for Wilmington, N.C. was swamped in a heavy storm off the Florida's east coast, near Miami. While the Ontario, the tugboat towing the barge, managed to rescue one man in the rough seas, and the barge sank. Supposedly the other four men had made it into a boat, but the Coast Guard cutter and the search plane found nothing the next day or the next. Sad thing was, Uncle Henry wasn't even scheduled to be on the boat. He had just been in port after unloading the barge load of sulfur when one of the seamen on the Northern Light quit. Henry decided to fill the last minute vacancy.

Uncle Henry lived in Mobile with his wife, Elvie. Others on Grandmother's side of the family lived there too. In listing the family members, one local article about the tragedy listed a "Mrs. R.H. Cochran" of New York City as one of Henry's sisters. That was Bessie. Even after she applied for the divorce she kept the last name of Cochran. Despite Henry's death, Aunt Elvie stayed close to our family. She was one of Jackie's favorites. Elvie was attractive and sophisticated and she and Jackie shared similar tastes in fashions and such. Mother, Jackie and Aunt Elvie would frequently to get together for a visit—and probably to go shopping.

It was around 1930, when Bessie became Jackie. She told others she picked the name out of a phone book. Maybe she liked Jacqueline because it sounded more sophisticated and modern than the homespun, old-fashioned name Bessie. An old family friend, Jennie Daw, is convinced Bessie chose Jacqueline out of her fondness for the preacher named Jack Hamilton who led the congregation—including the Pittman family—at the Hamilton Baptist Church back in Gateswood. She often signed her name "Jack" in the many letters she wrote to us before Mother died. Maybe she just changed her name hoping to change her luck. If so, it worked. She got a job working at the prestigious, swank Antoine's in New York City. Jackie was full of energy and unafraid of hard work. Our family had strong ethics regarding work and independence. Even during the Great Depression, when many of the area forests had disappeared and the mills closed, my father chose to work as a carpenter, painter and anything else he could do on his own, rather than accept a government subsidized job. That was his way.

When I said Jackie played hard, I should point out her idea of play set her apart from the other working girls. For her vacation in 1932 she wanted to learn to fly. An article in The New York Times read:

"Girl, 23, to be Air Pilot in 3 Weeks If Luck Holds"

Up betimes and out to an aviation field by 9 o'clock in the morning is a strange beginning to vacation days, when most working girls look forward to sleeping late during their weeks away from the job. But Jacqueline Cochrane (sic) has set herself the task this summer of becoming a licensed pilot in three weeks and she is working as hard to accomplish this as she did all winter to hold a job in a beauty shop, for there is a bet with a friend involved. She takes off in her plane as frequently as the instructors at Roosevelt Field will permit and hangs around the field picking up all the flying knowledge she can hear or observe. Back in her hotel room she spends her evenings studying rules and regulations for her Department of Commerce examination. She is having, she said today, the time of her life."

Billie Pittman Ayers and Beth Dees

Signed to her brother and his wife "To Ethel and Joe with Love, Jackie 1934," the same year Jackie entered the world's longest air race—the MacRobertson Air Race—from England to Australia.

Chapter Five: Jackie goes Solo

In her own handwritten notes in her papers at the Eisenhower Library in Abilene, Kansas, Aunt Jackie writes about being "the extra woman" invited to a social dinner given by friends and paired as a dinner partner with Floyd Odlum, to whom she was later married. She wrote, "The subject of flying came up during the dinner." She chatted with him about her plans to make big sales of dress patterns by traveling around the country. He said, part in jest, to beat the competition she would need to fly. She decided he was right. He bet her the cost of the lessons she couldn't learn to fly in less than three weeks. Three months was the usual time it took. She won that bet. Floyd probably knew she would. Jackie's passion for whatever she was doing, her impatience with pettiness, her directness would have given him clues. She told Mother and Grandmother the bet was that she learn in two weeks, not three, as the media reported. Either way, she won.

Jackie

"Some friend of mine one night said, 'Of all the things you want to do in your life what are you going to do?'" I said, "I'm going to do all these things' and I outlined my plans—definitely. Then they said, 'But you'd have to fly to do all that!' I responded, that sounds like a good idea."

In 1931 there were only 300 females licensed to fly. Amelia Earhart had been flying for a decade and only two months earlier had completed her solo flight across the

Atlantic. Flying was considered glamorous, exciting and a fast track to fame if you could win a big race, so learning to fly was more than just a young woman's whim. While others relaxed on vacation, Jackie, always the pragmatist, saw a purpose to this adventure of learning to fly. Not only would she win a bet, she would open herself to another world.

That first newspaper article about this young, attractive woman learning to fly was like a small ice cube, the core of a gigantic snowball that would grow through the years. Jackie was a great storyteller; she loved to laugh and she loved being the center of attention. She loved the limelight. So did Dad. We were audience to his jokes and stories at mealtimes.

Perhaps it was the flattering attention of these first few press interviews that lulled her into saying things she regretted, but never retracted. In that first news item when asked about her life she said her parents had died. In later articles Jackie described herself as 'orphan'. I want to believe her words were said innocently—not meaning to hurt anyone—just intending to make her story more interesting. I do believe she was soon swept up in the powerful attraction of fame. Once there, she could never bring herself to publicly admit the truth.

Aunt Jackie wasn't one to look back and try to make amends. She was unable to back up and face up to the truth. We all have weaknesses. We all want to look good, and it is hard to 'untell' a lie. Her shortcoming wasn't telling these first tiny untruths, her weakness was that she was never able to pull it out of herself to retract what she said about not having a family. That is sad to me, but it does not detract from who she was. Rather, it shows that she was human—like the rest of us. She still inspires me, as she

SUPERWOMAN Jacqueline Cochran

does other family members, and we still love her dearly. I have forgiven her for the wrong things she said about her family. And even if she wouldn't acknowledge us publicly, in private she let us know how much she cared for us.

Though some may have a hard time understanding this, her telling the media she was an orphan didn't create that much of a stir in my family. Or perhaps it just wasn't discussed in front of the children. We were familiar with Jackie's leanings toward drama. We knew her powerful ambitious drive made it easy for her to create her own stories. At the time, it just wasn't a big deal what she said, and even if it had been, none of us would have ever come out and contradicted her publicly. We were all living our own lives. We loved her. Besides we knew, and everyone she grew up with knew, and she knew, she wasn't an orphan. We ignored her comments. Instead we focused on her gutsy pluck, her flying and her other accomplishments. Later when her first autobiography came out, there were ripples in the family. In much later years Jerry, Aunt Mamie's oldest son, said his mother was treated for stomach ulcers after the book came out. But speaking for Mother, Dad and my brothers and sisters—no one mentioned what Jackie wrote in her book or said in public about the family. Over the years, I only know of three occasions where family members confronted her about what she told the public about her family. No major blow-ups: there were merely comments of disdain and annoyance than real confrontation. Conflict was not a family characteristic. No one was afraid of Jackie; we just did not want to hurt her in any way.

Jackie took easily to flying and loved it from the first. As far as I know, no one else in my family was interested in flying. Years later, in a rare newspaper interview,

Grandmother answered a reporter who asked if she had ever flown with her famous pilot daughter.

"No, I haven't," said Mrs. Pittman "I'm scared to death of those things. I sat in the front seat of one of Jackie's planes once. You know I never even saw her fly until she landed on Walton (County) soil two years ago."

I have never been fond of flying myself. It is not that I am afraid of it, I just get airsick easily and so stay on the ground whenever possible. The last time I flew, however, it was cross-country to a ceremony honoring Jackie and I had no trouble either way.

Her first instructor, Husky Lewellyn, said Jackie was a natural pilot. He later said, "She was a born flyer, one of the smartest gals in the air I ever saw." On August 17, 1932 the United States Department of Commerce issued Jackie Private Pilot's License #26465. Other New York newspapers followed up on the story of the young woman learning to fly so fast.

"If ambition has anything to do with successful flights I'm going to make a name for myself—I'm chock full of it," the 26-year-old told a New York newspaper reporter in 1932. Jackie was a great talker but she meant every word.

By learning to fly, Jacqueline not only won money to continue her flying lessons she also began what was to be a life-long symbiotic relationship with the press. There were few exceptions. During WWII years when Jackie was lobbying to get the Women's Air Service Pilots organization recognized as part of the military, *The New York Time's* Drew Pearson called her "manipulative" and "a glamour girl" in his well-read column. But, the press generally treated her with respect. And it was returned. Jackie was generous with interviews, careful to return calls and on the occasion of press conferences, more than once; arranged details, such as refreshments.

Within two weeks of her getting her pilot's license Jackie quit her job at Antoine's, packed her bags and drove West across the country to California. She planned to make a career out of flying and in her words, "Winter was coming on which would interfere with daily flying in New York, and I had no time to waste."

In San Diego at Lindbergh Field, she trained seriously, learning the other fundamentals of flying. Within three months she applied for and received her limited commercial pilot's license. Always the businesswoman, Jackie realized the money she was paying out to rent the planes would be better spent in paying for her own plane. She managed to buy a Waco. Along with instruction at Ryan Flying School, Jackie learned from everyone she could. A man the family always believed to be Jackie's first true love, Ted Marshall, also helped her learn to fly. He was a flight lieutenant in the Navy, and she probably met him earlier in Pensacola. She wrote Mother letters about him. When he was stationed in San Diego, he helped teach her flying skills, using the same rigid course of training used for the naval students in Pensacola. When the weather warmed up and summer began, she flew back East. Selling her first airplane and her automobile, she ordered a new four-seater Waco. Within a year, she had earned the transport license, giving her three of the five pilot licenses available.

Suddenly, with her new wings, we were not so far away. She wrote my mother and dad that she wanted to come home to visit. She asked them to keep the visit a secret but to please have Daddy check the local airstrip and make sure it was in good shape.

Billie Pittman Ayers and Beth Dees

Aunt Jackie grew up in a large caring family. We made a point of taking care of one another. In my family, Mother and Dad went beyond even that. Our home was like a hotel. As we grew into teenagers our mother never—or rarely—knew how many places to set at the table or how many of our friends she would find sleeping on her floors in the morning. They were always welcome and everyone loved her for her quiet loving spirit. It was not unusual for friends to stay at our house, sometimes an entire summer. I always thought it was because it was such a pleasant place to be. Mother and Daddy took care of a lot of people, including Jackie when she was a young woman, plus other relatives. When we later moved to Marianna in 1936, Grandmother's permanent home was with my family for the rest of her life. As she got older, my dad took care of her, except when she would take trips to visit her other children in California. I really don't know how my parents did what they did—financially or otherwise.

We were so excited about getting to see Jackie. I was about six years old the first time she flew home to see us. She was always so much fun. When she got there she lined all the children up and told us matter-of-factly, "I have changed my name so don't call me Aunt Bessie anymore. You're to call me Aunt Jackie from now on." That was fine with us. It didn't bother us one bit.

By now, Jackie's mother had remarried a widower from Ponce De Leon, named Jim Jackson. Mr. Jackson owned a big 160-acre farm in Knox Hill, east of DeFuniak Springs, and they lived in a large log home with a hallway open to the outside, running through the middle. They lived in one side of the house and rented out the other to the Gardners. It was certainly a different kind of marriage than the one Grandmother shared with Ira. Grandmother didn't even change her last name; neither did she live with Mr. Jackson (as we called him) all the time. Sometimes she stayed for months at The Florida Hotel on the lake yard in DeFuniak Springs. Madge Rutherford, the hotel owner's daughter, remembers Grandmother getting monthly checks in the mail from Jackie to pay her bills. Grandmother didn't have a checking account and would cash checks at Warren's Drugstore. Mary Caroline Warren Murray said her father proudly passed on Jacqueline's checks around to show the traveling salesmen who stopped to call at the pharmacy. By now everybody knew who Jackie was.

Ed Rushing, one of Mr. Jackson's grandsons, still lives within a few miles of the Jackson home place. The house is gone. Mr. Rushing married young Nettie Mae Gardner, whose father had farmed with his grandfather, Jim Jackson. Mr. Rushing never said he met Jacqueline when she came to Knox Hill to visit Grandmother, but Nettie Mae did.

"She was a nice-looking lady and nice to everyone that come along," said Nettie Mae, now 91. My mother thought a lot of her. Her mother would tell my mother, "My daughter is coming to visit and I want y'all to come over and meet her…. and we did…she brought her mother clothes and she gave me a little colored belt once."

Grandmother already had more clothes than she could ever wear, but any time Jackie came to visit, she would bring her outfits to wear. Sometimes the gifts were simple—dresses, blouses, a sweater—other gifts were extravagant, such as a chinchilla fur coat.

A year later Jackie flew back to visit. This time we didn't have to keep it a secret and soon, everyone in town knew she was coming. Bessie had left town in the late 1920s, depressed over her tragedies. She returned with her head high, a new name, and a growing reputation—this time as a respected aviatrix and businesswoman. No matter what opinion they had previously held of her, a crowd of townspeople turned up at the landing strip several miles east of town on what was called "Blueberry Hill" to watch the 26-year-old fly in. It really wasn't a landing strip. It was just a stretch of flat cleared ground. In a letter to Mother, Jackie asked her to have Dad take a close look at the strip to make sure it was mowed and the ground was firm.

Seven-year-old Mary Caroline Warren was among those who showed up for the homecoming. Her family was prominent in town; not only did her father own Warren Pharmacy—that is still in business today under the name Service Drugs—her grandfather owned almost an entire city block, which included a theatre, a carousel, restaurant and more.

Today Mrs. Murray lives in a large ante-bellum home on Circle Drive surrounded by exquisite antiques, dark molding and ticking antique clocks. "I went with my parents," said Mary Caroline, who later married into the Murrays. "A lot of people went out to see her fly in. It was a big deal for the town. That was really something for a woman to fly. Even airplanes were a rarity. …When she got out of her plane I could see she was wearing all white. She had a white scarf around her neck and she had on jodhpurs. I had never seen a lady in jodhpurs before. I thought she was beautiful. I didn't know if she impressed anyone else, but she sure impressed me," said Mrs. Murray.

Aware of the town's earlier opinion of Jackie, Murray said her family was more impressed with Jackie's 'get-up-and-go'. "We thought she really pulled herself up by her bootstraps," said Mrs. Murray. "We all admired her for that."

SUPERWOMAN Jacqueline Cochran

Some DeFuniak residents who knew her claimed they always knew she would make something of herself. "You could see she had something different about her," said one of the town's three phone operators in the late 1920s. Other residents said she never seemed different from anyone else in the small country town. "She was shy and I was shy," was the way Ausborne Johnson of Tallahassee remembers her. He met her when he was 19 and ran the "Top of the Hill" grocery and cafe on Highway No. 1, now Highway 90, going west out of DeFuniak Springs.

"Every Sunday morning, real early, she would come in to buy three boxes of snuff for her mother. Three for 25¢. She was older. I never did really say anything to her but I always took my time getting the snuff out of the glass case. It was down low and I would have to bend over to get it and I can remember being able to look at her legs though the glass. Of course at the time she wasn't anybody special and I couldn't believe it in later years when somebody told me that this girl I knew from DeFuniak Springs had become the famous Jacqueline Cochran."

Another DeFuniak resident, Mary Lee Ellisor, said she didn't go to the airstrip but got to see Jackie dressed in her flying regalia because the Pittmans lived next door. "Mother didn't want us gawking and wouldn't let us go outside," said Mrs. Ellisor. "We had to watch from the windows."

Chapter Six: Gwen's Bird's Eye View

My mother helped my sister Gwen pack a suitcase. What could a 13-year-old girl need for a summer-long trip around the country? Everything. Aunt Jackie's plane was small. There wouldn't be much room. Never having been in a plane before, Gwen was excited, nervous and already practically famous among her school friends, including her good friend—Helen Betty Harbeson, whose grandfather owned Harbeson Mill in town. The friends studied a map and plotted out the trip. Gwen had never really been away from home. To be invited to spend the summer with her Aunt Jackie, flying around the country was the best summer vacation she could dream of! Gwen who passed away in March of '97 told, in her own words, about that summer ...

"Actually it had been Myrtle's daughter—Willie Mae—who was originally supposed to go, but for some reason, Aunt Jackie changed her mind and I went instead. She flew into DeFuniak Springs to get me in her small Waco. First, she took us (the children) to town and bought us all new shoes and she also bought me some new dresses and a hat.

The day came when she and I were to leave. All the family and lot of people from town went to the airport—it was really just a grass runway—there were no buildings. It was a cloudy day but we had no way of knowing what the weather was ahead of us. We were gone only a short while when we had to turn back because of bad weather. As soon as the storm passed, we took off again and our first stop was Pensacola. We landed at the Naval Air Station. Just before landing I became deathly air sick. Aunt Jackie pleaded with me to hold it, saying we would be on the ground in just a few minutes. I couldn't. That was the only time I got airsick.

"We made that cross-country trip in her Waco plane. She had it painted a special green. I'll never forget it. She wanted to have that particular color of paint named 'Cochran Green,' but that's one wish she didn't get.

Mr. Bill Taylor flew with us from Pensacola to Omaha, Nebraska. I was sitting in back of Aunt Jackie when suddenly her parachute fell off into my lap. This was very frightening because this left us with only one parachute. Aunt Jackie told Mr. Taylor if anything happened he was to take me and jump. She said she would rather die than have to face my parents if anything should happen to me. Thank God nothing went wrong and we landed safely in Omaha.

It was just outside Salt Lake City, Utah where the Waco actually did go down. Downdrafts from off the nearby mountain range kept the small plane from gaining altitude to make it over them and soon Jackie decided she was going to have to put the plane down in the dirt rather than risk flying into the face of the mountain.

She told me we were going to have to land. There was a farm below and we headed for it. Cattle were grazing in a very large field and we flew over it several times trying to frighten them into running into just one area of the field. After this failed, our only alternative was to land in a wheat field we spotted nearby. Jackie flew low over this area, but we could not determine if there were irrigation ditches or not. She told me to brace myself because she was going to land, stop the plane quickly and we might possibly end up landing on the top side of the plane. Being the expert pilot she was, the plane stopped on its nose, tail high in the air. We got out of the plane as soon as possible. A farmer had been watching us circle overhead and was by our sides within minutes after we landed. We were taken to a farmhouse and given a very nice lunch. I have never seen a cleaner house in my life. I was only 13, but this stands out in my mind. The lady of the house had us lie down and rest while she and her husband contacted a lady who lived some distance away to ask her to take us into Salt Lake City. Aunt Jackie was upset when the lady finally arrived. She had her entire family with her and there was hardly room for our luggage and us. But we managed somehow to get everything in and we started for the city. The lady charged $50, which in 1933 was highway robbery, plus we were so crowded. We checked in at the Hotel Utah where this same lady made many, many calls telling everyone about her experience. It wasn't the first time, nor would it be the last Jackie would walk away from a wreck. But it was the first and last time for me.

Things went from bad to worse. While on the ground waiting for repairs Jackie found out that her friend, Ted Marshall, who had helped her learn to fly, had been killed in a plane wreck. In a rush, Jackie made arrangements for me to stay at a hotel in Utah while she flew in a commercial plane out to California for the funeral. Jackie remained close friends with Ted's parents and his family throughout her life and often visited them at their home, which was only several miles from her estate. On another day of bad weather we landed in Chicago in a whirlwind. We were the only plane to land that day, but she had to land because we were low on fuel. Floyd Odlum was with us, but he and Jackie didn't want anyone to know, so he jumped out on the runway so it looked like we were the only two people in the plane. By then men had run out of the hangar to help because the winds from the approaching storm were so strong they were threatening to flip the plane. A couple of men even lay on the wings to help stabilize the craft while they moved it into the protective hangar. Floyd later met with us and we continued the trip.

We were also in a terrible storm in Cheyenne, Wyoming and that night I offered to rub Aunt Jackie's legs because she said they were hurting her so bad...I guess from fighting with the plane. She said told me that was the nicest thing anybody ever did for her.

We flew to Colorado, then to California and on to New York. We stayed in California for a while. Aunt Jackie was fun to be with. She bought me several pretty outfits. We stayed in the Ambassador Hotel. It cost about a hundred dollars a day, which was like a million dollars to me. I sat in the lobby watching all the movie stars go by. That was pretty heady stuff for a 13-year-old girl from the country. She finally sent me home from New York by train before school started. I didn't ever want that trip to end.

If I had been my mother I wouldn't have let me go...because Jackie was too young and she didn't have that much experience flying. But she was a good pilot. I was probably the first child to fly cross-country in a private plane. That's my record."

One other memory from that trip with Aunt Jackie stands out in Gwen's mind. "It was the year Aunt Jackie came to DeFuniak Springs to take me with her to California. One day we went to the cemetery to visit her son's—Robert Cochran, Junior's grave. I remember her stooping down over the grave, crying pitifully. She stood up, said 'If only he had lived, my life would be so different,' and then ran off into a wooded area. My daddy ran after her and with his arms around her brought her back to the gravesite. We got back in the cars and left."

Gwen was the first in our family to meet Jackie's friend, Floyd Bostwick Odlum, the man she would later marry. During that summer, he met with Jackie and my sister Gwen several times, sometimes traveling by train and periodically flying with them from one stop to another. Our mother said Jackie told her she met Floyd at a party in Miami. Mother said Jackie was working and had volunteered to deliver a package to this swank dinner party. The hostess invited her in. Floyd met and fell in love with her. Or maybe she did with him. Maybe it was a mutual attraction. Floyd was the friend she had made the bet with, about learning to fly in three weeks. Through her own hard work, she had already begun improving her financial status, but flying was, and still is an expensive hobby. Floyd was instrumental in providing financial support for her flight training and Jackie's races from the beginning until the end.

By the time they met at the party, Floyd B. Odlum was already a multi-millionaire and the president of the vast Atlas Corporation. He was fourteen years older than Jackie. A couple of years later, Floyd divorced his wife, Hortense McQuarrie who was president of Bonwit Teller.

A year later, in 1936, on Jackie's favorite date—her birthday—May 11, he married Jackie in a quiet ceremony in Kingman, Arizona.

Floyd's devotion to Jackie was intense and lifelong. He was her Prince Charming and he treated her like a princess. In a scrapbook he gave her on her birthday before they married, he wrote, "To 'Lucky Strike' on her birthday/1934 with every expectation that this book will be filled with all sorts of good things about her." And it was.

Although he was a self-made-millionaire by age 30 and one the country's most powerful entrepreneurs, Floyd, like Jackie, started with little. His father, a Methodist minister, never made more than $800 a year. Floyd worked to put himself through law school and passed the Colorado State Bar exam in 1914. His first job was in the legal department of Utah Power & Light, making $50 a month. Within three years, his company sent him to New York City to represent it in a law firm. Two years later he joined the law firm and quickly became vice-president. He and his good friend, George Howard, pooled about $40,000 to speculate in utility investments. Floyd guessed right when he sold out of the stock market and converted his holdings to cash right before the crash in 1929. Others took a financial beating that year, while Floyd managed to raise $9 million in that year alone. Using this, he went after scores of companies with suffering trust funds. He earned the nickname '50% Odlum' by buying up other companies' stock at that rate. Within five years, Odlum's Atlas Corporation had overtaken 22 investment companies; including several of the big players; Sterling Securities Corporation, Goldman Sachs Trading Company and the Chatham Phoenix Allied Corporation. He reorganized businesses as diverse as banking, railroads, department stores, public utilities and motion pictures. By then his $14 million ballooned into $100 million.

Not only did Floyd adore Aunt Jackie, she was his main hobby. Going after the speed, altitude and distance records and entering air races cost serious money. He was more than happy to back her up. He urged her on.

In 1934 Jackie entered her first big air race—the MacRobertston Race. It happened to be the world's longest air race, 12,000 miles from England to Australia. Her Gee Bee, the name stood for the Granville Brothers who built it, was one of 20 planes that took off from the Mildenhall Airdrome on the morning of October 21. Only three of the planes entered were from America. Jackie liked attention, but she was unprepared for the tremendous onslaught of publicity the flyers received. When one of the English newspapers referred to her as a "manicurist ...who would be only a passenger on the flight," in a follow-up article she responded in her to-become-famous steely, blunt style.

"It is incorrect to say that I am merely a manicurist in America," she said. "I am a business woman. I am prepared to produce all my flying documents and they will show that I have done more than 1000 hours flying and that on three occasions I have made solo crossings of the American continent. I also hold No. 21 transport license in our country, and I have done many hours of night flying and made night landings."

Only half way across Europe, Jackie and her co-pilot Wesley Smith were forced to land in Bucharest, Rumania, because of engine problems. Even landing became a potential life or death situation when the air flaps on the wings malfunctioned. One flap would stick up, the other down, seriously affecting the plane's balance. The plane was so noisy they couldn't even hear each other so Wesley wrote a note to Jackie, while she was trying to land, suggesting they fly over the landing strip and bail out. She wrote back for him to go ahead if he wanted, but it was her plane and she was going to get it down. On the third try, they touched down and used every inch of the long runway stopping the plane. Jackie was bitterly disappointed to be out of the race. But that adventure wasn't over. In the middle of the next night, while taking the Orient Express to Paris, she ran into another problem. At a loud knocking on her door, she opened it to find several officials standing there in a threatening manner asking for her passport. Unfortunately, they didn't speak English and Jackie didn't speak Hungarian. She produced the document, remembering with dismay as she did, that in her hurry to get everything ready for the race she did not get it stamped for legal entry to Rumania. If the race had gone as planned she would have only been there for as long as one air plane stop. When they saw it wasn't stamped they grabbed her arm and were about to drag her from the train. She suddenly remembered in her handbag she had a newspaper article published that very day showing her posing with Rumania's Air Force Minister. They looked at it carefully, and then left. The next morning she learned they had been looking for a jewel thief who just so happened to match a description of Jackie. Jackie was so upset over the string of events she wrote home to talk with Mother about her bad luck. We worried about her.

Billie Pittman Ayers and Beth Dees

13-year-old Gwen said the summer spent with her Aunt Jackie was a high point of her life, plus she also felt she set her own personal record as the first child to fly cross-country. (use of photo courtesy of Carl Bigelow with the *Oakland Tribune*).

Chapter Seven: Paradise in the Desert

Aunt Jackie had a big heart and thoroughly loved doing for others. After we moved to Marianna in 1936, she sent us boxes filled with gifts: clothes, cosmetics, hats and always at Christmas time she sent boxes of California dates. She wrote frequently to my mother, sending her newspaper clippings, updating us on her races and awards. Mother kept many of these family letters and photos in a built-in seat beneath a large window in our home. My father died in 1972, two years after Mother and the house was sold. The treasured packet of family letters and memorabilia stored in the window seat was overlooked. Our parents' deaths were the most devastating time of my and my sibling's life. Material things were not thought of. Later, the house was torn down. I am still sick about losing these family treasures but I am grateful for those my sister, Gwen, kept and gave to me.

Jackie helped pay for or loan money for the education of at least two of her nephews. Whenever there was a medical or other family financial crisis, she was ready to help.

Jackie's generosity extended well beyond family. When I went to California in 1996 to attend ceremonies honoring Jackie and the new commemorative 50 cents air mail stamp created in her honor, a young man, Jamie Montenegro, walked up and introduced himself. He said he grew up on Jackie's ranch where his mother had worked in Jackie's home and his father had been a groundskeeper. His parents, Paul and Sylvia, were in the crowd and he found them and introduced them to me. He told how Jackie had made it possible for him to follow his dream and become an archeologist by paying for his college education. The affection and admiration they had for Jackie was obvious.

Glennis Yeager, wife of General Chuck Yeager, remembers Jackie opening her vast closets to her and other close friends and giving away expensive dresses and fashions she had brought back with her from shopping sprees at the fashion shows in Paris.

Jackie's generous nature revealed itself also in her involvement with many charities and service organizations. With her husband's help, she organized a private foundation—the Cochran-Odlum Foundation—through which they made sizable donations to a number of worthy causes, among them the National Arthritis Foundation, of which Floyd once served as president. Floyd suffered terribly from a degenerative arthritis.

When I was about 15, Aunt Jackie sent me a pair of jodhpurs I thought were simply beautiful. I felt quite stylish in them, riding my horse with my friends after school. Sometimes the clothes she sent us would be too fancy to wear in the casual, comfortable atmosphere of Marianna, so Mother would cut them up and sew them into something else. She even tailored a suit for my brother Gordon from fabric Jackie sent. After Aunt Jackie started her cosmetics company in 1935, she would send large laboratory sized jars of ointments, lotions and bottles of her perfumes. I still have a bottle of her cologne "Pursuit" from her "Wings To Beauty" line. Even Dad would let us give him a facial with the complexion soaps and moisturizing creams she sent.

Aunt Jackie and my dad were so much alike. I know I was the subject of one of their worst arguments. Jackie wanted to adopt me when I was about five years old. I guess she thought we were all family and since she lost her only son, maybe she thought since there were so many of us, Mom and Dad wouldn't mind sharing. But if that was what she thought, she was wrong. Of course, my dad said no. I remember them wrangling about it until the air was blue, which meant Dad's 'colorful' language he learned in his seafaring days came back to help him express his anger that she would even suggest such a thing. Many years later, I learned Jackie had also approached her brother-in-law, Will Alford about adopting their daughter, Joyce. She had also approached Willie Mae to ask if she could adopt Willie Mae's daughter, Mildred, when she was between the ages of two and three. In later years she did adopt children, or rather adopt an entire orphanage. Mother said it was in Arizona.

In 1935 she asked her family—everyone—to move to be with her in California. She wanted us closer and she helped pay for the big move. Jackie thought of the novel idea of renting an entire Pullman train car to bring her mother, siblings and their families and all of their belongings out to her. I had just turned nine years old when we moved across the country. Two other more distant family members came with us: Jewell Boswell, Will's half sister and Silas Edward Ingram, we called him Uncle Sy, —from my Mother's side of the family. She paid for a Ford pickup truck so my father and Aunt Mamie and Aunt Myrtle's husband could drive out to California ahead of everyone else and prepare. They made the trip in June and converted the back of the pick-up into sleeping quarters for the nights along the way.

My younger brother, Gordon Pittman, was only five years old when we made the cross-country trip. He still chuckles today when he thinks of the row Grandmother got into with the conductor. He tells it like this:

Billie Pittman Ayers and Beth Dees

"When the train pulled into the depot at DeFuniak Springs, the three families were lined up waiting. Grandmother was at the head of the line. Grandmother could talk the 'horns off a Billy goat' as the old expression goes. When the conductor, tickets in hand, counted us onto the train, instead of going in first, she stepped beside him and 'helped' him count…one, two, three…Somewhere down the line, she got one number ahead of him. There was quite a crowd of us! He called all of us off the train and began the count again…one, two, three. Once more, Grandmother got ahead of him in the count and once more he called us off the train. After the same thing happened the third time, in exasperation, he shouted, 'Go on, get on the train! If someone rides free to California, I can't help it."

Gordon also tells about the train stopping at the Mississippi River because the bridge was not yet finished.

"We were allowed to get off the train and stretch our legs while they "broke" the train into separate cars which crossed the river on a ferry. That's when I remember seeing a trainman who held the longest flashlight I had ever seen. He spotted me, walked over and said, 'Sonny, would you like to see my magic flashlight move this train?' I nodded, eyes large, as he said, 'Watch. When I shine the beam from the flashlight on the wheels of this car it will move.' And it did! I thought my eyes would pop out of my head. Of course, I paid no attention to the puffing of the engine as it moved the cars into place."

Jackie hired our father to help build the large 7,600-square-foot main ranch for her and her soon-to-be husband Floyd. It was a treat for me to ride with Dad to Needles, a small town near Indio, to pick out the stones for the huge fireplace planned for the living room at the ranch. Dad was well suited for the job of building the ranch. He was multitalented—having supported his family as a builder, bricklayer, carpenter, painter, millwright and engineer. We lived nearby on a fruit ranch with groves of oranges, grapefruits, dates and about forty acres of grapes and we had a milk cow and chickens. While the ranch was being built, Jackie often brought many visitors to our home, including Floyd. My brother and I remember how every time they visited, Jackie would go into the refrigerator, skim the cream off the fresh milk, pour it over crumbled bread and feed it—spoonful by spoonful—to Floyd. It was so sweet how Jackie doted on Floyd. We had a Native American, Ben, who helped with farm chores and was very good to us. And there was Bear, a lovable watchdog, so big the smaller kids could ride him like a horse.

Jackie lived in an apartment in Los Angeles while her ranch was being built. She often came to check on the building of her ranch and stayed with us. And we visited her in her apartment in LA.

After Jacqueline and Floyd married in 1936 and moved to their ranch, there were always people coming and going. Jackie and Floyd seemed to know everyone. In the following years, visitors to the ranch included outstanding people in every aspect of life, from movie stars to rocket scientists. Among them were: General James Doolittle, Bob Hope, Dr. Edward Teller, Samuel Goldwyn, Rosalind Russell, Janet Gaynor, Merle Oberon, Gloria Swanson, Roy Wilkings, Jules Stein, Dr. Norman Vincent Peal, Jinx Falkenberg McCrary, Walt Disney, Madame Chiang Kai-shek, Gov. Nelson A. Rockefeller, Jascha Heiftz, Igor Sikorsky, James Cagney, Madeleine Carroll and Prince Victor Emmanuel and that does not even include the United States presidents who came to visit. I believe of all the notables who came out, Jackie still most enjoyed having other pilots out to visit, since her favorite topic was ... flying.

The ranch was a whopping 732 acres in Coachella Valley, which is in Southeastern California, below Los Angeles. It became an oasis in the desert with flowers and fruit trees everywhere. Standing outside the house, by the large, heated swimming pool, you could see a distant range of mountains, then off to the West—the much larger snow-capped San Jacinto Mountain. Looking down the hill from the main house, you could see manicured groves of citrus trees, giant date palms and the vineyards. Uncle "Sy" remained with Jackie for years and helped to plant and look after the groves. After we moved back to Florida from California, Aunt Jackie never forgot to send us boxes of dates every Christmas. We loved them so much, I guess because you couldn't find fresh-picked dates like that in the grocery store then.

Floyd described the ranch in a letter inviting President and Mrs. Eisenhower to stay at the ranch while President Eisenhower recovered after minor surgery. He wrote:

"Miss Cochran and I invite you to use our ranch ...and would be highly honored by your acceptance. We believe the ranch may have some advantages over other places, considering the season and the circumstances...

The days will be warm but not hot, the nights cool but not cold (perhaps down to 60 degrees F) and the skies are almost constantly clear. Our main house is segregated on a hummock from the other houses. A warmed swimming pool is only thirty feet away across the lawn from the entrance to the house. The house itself has a large double bedroom with dressing room and bath, a single bedroom with bath, a maid's room with bath, a library (that has its dressing room and bath and therefore could be made into another bedroom if desired), besides the living room, dining room and card room. There is equipment for projection of 35 mm pictures.

...For light exercise we have an English croquet court and a putting green as well as a range for skeet and trap shooting. There is also a nine-hole golf course. We have both electric and gasoline carts to go anywhere around the property and up and down the main house hummock.

Close by the main house, but off the hummock, a distance of perhaps 100 feet, is a three-room cottage that probably would be ideal for your Mother. Next to it are two additional double bedrooms with baths. Then, on a separate hummock, we have what we call our main guesthouse with a large living room, kitchen and two double bedrooms, each with bath. That house is about 200 feet from the main hummock. On three other hummocks, a little more distance from the main house but no more than one-third of a mile away, we have three more available guesthouses. ...

The houses I've mentioned are somewhat isolated from each other on their separate hummocks and all of them are surrounded first by lawns and then by date, grapefruit and tangerine groves."

Mrs. Eisenhower declined that particular invitation from Floyd, but the Eisenhowers did stay at the Cochran-Odlum ranch on many other occasions including Christmas Eve 1961. After President Eisenhower left office, they spent more than a year there, staying in one of the guesthouses while he worked on his memoirs. He also loved to paint and presented Jackie and Floyd with one of his works of art. Others are on display at the Dwight D. Eisenhower Library in Abilene, Kansas. I've seen them and think they are quite good.

The ranch may have been in the middle of the desert but it was anything but quiet. Aunt Jackie loved to entertain and was a wonderful gourmet cook. Of course she had plenty of help when she gave dinner parties. I loved the way she dressed for those dinner parties. Even at my young age, I could see she was strikingly beautiful.

I must have been about nine-years-old when Aunt Jackie called me, Gordon and the other kids in one evening to introduce us to her guests at a dinner party she gave in her large LA apartment. Howard Hughes and Amelia Earhart came together to the dinner party. Mother and Grandmother were among the six or eight other guests. Aunt Jackie always brought the children in to meet her guests after the adults had enjoyed their meal. We had our own good time eating our supper in the apartment's breakfast room, off the kitchen prior to the dinner party. Unfortunately my main memory of that particular evening was one of embarrassment because a strap on a pair of brand new sandals I was wearing had broken. Woods, Jackie's chauffeur, had taken Mother and me shopping that day and she bought me a beautiful pair of multi-colored sandals. When one of the guests commented on them, I looked down and saw one of the straps was broken. I was mortified and ran out of the room. Such things can be terribly important to little girls.

I know Jackie stayed up late with those dinner parties but somehow she was always up and ready to talk and talk and talk with me the morning after.

Aunt Jackie was naturally attractive, but she didn't leave her beauty to chance. Like everything else, she worked at it. She considered attaining and sustaining beauty to be a worthy effort. She thought every woman should look at it the same way. In a magazine article she wrote, "A woman, to accomplish all she can, must present herself at an absolute peak of attractiveness, just as she must keep herself in good health and her brain growing and alert. Her beauty is not a frivolous irrelevancy but a touchstone to a full life."

Margaret Ann Currlin Clark, a secretary for Jackie, said Jackie spent considerable time every morning preparing her appearance. When Ms, Clark arrived for work, Jackie would have her sit on the bed and take dictation while Jackie continued styling her hair or applying makeup. However, Jackie was also known to say, "Vanity is time-consuming," and prompted women to spend no more than 15 minutes a day to look their best.

Racing airplanes wasn't exactly a delicate feminine hobby, but Jacqueline often would step out of an airplane after a race looking as if she had just stepped out of a beauty parlor instead. More than once she kept the press waiting on the runway after a race, while she touched up her makeup and on more than one occasion, she changed in the back of the plane out of her flying togs into a stylish dress or other fresh outfit before emerging.

It's no wonder Jackie ended up marrying one of the country's top businessmen. She was an entrepreneur at heart and in 1953 she was named the "Woman of the Year in Business" by an Associated Press editors' poll. She wrote in her second autobiography how, even in her early years in New York, she invested in several beauty salons where the services were considerably cheaper than Antoine's. As with everything else, she felt she knew a better way of doing things, which in many cases was quite true. She wanted to make her own beauty formulas so in 1935 she hired a top chemist, perfume consultant and opened a small office and laboratory in Roselle, New

Jersey. Jacqueline Cochran Cosmetics was formed and, because of sales, was included in the list of top Fortune 1000 companies.

Jackie did nothing by halves and she wasn't content to follow the crowd on what had been developed in the cosmetics industry. She was a pioneer even in the world of beauty. Her chemist helped her develop the first greaseless moisturizer. Called "Flowing Velvet", it became quite popular nationally. Jacqueline Cochran Cosmetics also developed formulas for lipsticks, antiperspirants, perfumes and new hair color dyes. She flew thousands of miles, after the war ended, promoting her skin care line appropriately named "Wings to Beauty." Another popular item she designed for travel was called the "Perk-Up" cylinder. This three-and-a-half inch stick came apart into six sections that held everything: cleansing cream, foundation, eye shadow, rouge, solid perfume and a sifter for face powder. She also was the American distributor for several famous French perfumes, most notably Nina Ricci.

And then there were the clothes. Aunt Jackie loved beautiful clothes. She would fly to Paris to the hottest fashion shows and buy outfits right off the runway. Everything—from creating the perfect moisturizer to perfecting a jet wing's shape—was a challenge to Jackie. She enjoyed sharing her interests and answers with others. And she did it with great enthusiasm and energy. In a usual week she might write an article for a teen magazine advising on the appropriate shade and use of lipstick, give a public speech about the safety of commercial airlines, grant a lengthy interview to an aviation magazine providing technical details on a recent record she had set and then end it by flying cross country to get in a few rounds of golf with friends.

Jackie's second husband, Floyd B. Odlum (far left) was one of America's richest and most powerful men following the Depression. Dwight D. Eisenhower visited the Odlum-Cochran ranch in California many times and even had a small guest cottage many times he worked in for months while writing his memoirs.

Chapter Eight: The Bendix…Super bowl of the Air Races

Aunt Jackie wanted to fly in The Bendix Transcontinental Air Race. Air Races were as popular then as American college football games are today and the Bendix was the Super Bowl. In the summer of 1935 eight of the country's top male fliers were preparing for the Bendix, one of the world's toughest annual air races. Starting in Los Angeles it ended 2,042 miles to the east in Cleveland, Ohio. Just getting in the race was a battle because a female had never entered the race. After race officials told her 'no,' Jackie approached each male competitors individually and talked them into signing a waiver agreeing to compete with her. Then another obstacle popped up. Right before the race, representatives for the plane's manufacturer—Norththrop—told Jackie they were dissatisfied with the plane's performance in preliminary flights. She didn't want to drop out. She put them on the spot, asking if they wanted to say publicly state there was a problem with the plane. They said no. She told them she intended to compete in it.

Fog began rolling in off the Atlantic just before her 3 a.m. take-off time. The plane ahead of Jackie's disappeared into the thick gray mist. There was an explosion. The plane crashed just beyond the end of the runway, killing the pilot. Feeling sick, Jackie waited while the wreckage was cleared. A race official walked up and tried to talk her out of flying, arguing the fog and her heavy fuel load made it too dangerous. Everyone was nervous and, again, the Northrop officials asked her to reconsider dropping out of the race.

SUPERWOMAN Jacqueline Cochran

She quietly called Floyd. Although he must have been concerned for her safety, he didn't tell her what to do. Instead, he told her, "There is a fine line between a course of action based on logic, and one to satisfy an emotional urge, and that no one could draw that line for another." They hung up. Bypassing her logic, she decided to satisfy that emotional urge and she climbed up in her plane and took off. After all that preparation and traumatic decision-making, she didn't even get to finish the race. But she did start it. At daybreak, she landed in Kingman, Arizona. Asked what happened, she made no excuses. She didn't say complain about the problems with the airplane. She said flat out she just got tired and quit. Looking back on that race, she said she felt if she had failed to start in that race, she's not sure she would have ever raced again.

The following year her plans for the Bendix in 1936 fell apart literally when the plane she planned to fly broke in half during a landing after the engine quit. A week earlier the plane caught fire in flight and had been repaired. That year, Louise Thaden won the Bendix, the first woman to do so.

In the fall of 1937 Jackie's luck improved and she set a new Woman's International Speed Record flying a Seversky plane. In December she set another new record flying from New York to Miami in only 4 hours and 12 minutes. This thrilled the plane's designer and manufacturer, Alexander P. Seversky. Until then, he had been unsuccessful in getting the United States Army to consider buying his P-35 plane. Seversky was convinced if Jackie would fly his P-35 in the 1938 Bendix and win; it would make the plane's reputation. It happened just that way. She made headlines across the country and back home in DeFuniak Springs. The headline in the September 9 issue of the DeFuniak paper read:

> "DeFuniak Woman Wins Bendix Derby. Former resident here wins from 12, Los Angeles to Cleveland."

The story went on to say.

> "The woman who won from twelve men in the more than two thousand mile Los Angeles-to-Cleveland air derby to win the Bendix award (not that she needed the money) is a DeFuniak product. Jacqueline Cochrane (nee Bessie Pittman) now the wife of Floyd B. Odlum, a California multimillionaire, lived in DeFuniak Springs for a considerable length of time, leaving here something like twelve or fifteen years ago, and took up the flying game under the name which she won the Bendix trophy."

Several area residents complained anonymously in the newspaper that Jackie fudged beyond reason in the national media about her age and other basic facts about her life.

> "I see that some of the newspapers referred to her as a 'red-haired orphan girl,'" one woman was quoted. "How do they get that way? She's not redheaded, or she wasn't when she left here and she's not an orphan yet—her mother is still living (Miss Cochran's mother, who has re-married since the family's return from California is living on a farm near DeFuniak Springs) and she herself, was a

mother before her father died. If she's a red-haired orphan girl, then I'm Helen of Troy."

Despite the disgruntlement over Jackie's stories, DeFuniak relaxed its harsh opinion of her, formed when she lived there, and began claiming Jackie as being 'one of them'. They boasted about her in the DeFuniak newspaper and among themselves. But Jackie no longer considered herself to be 'one of them'. She never mentioned DeFuniak Springs to anyone. It was a taboo subject, like her former husband Robert Cochran and her lost child, Robert Cochran, Jr. When she referred to her early years in her autobiographies and in speeches and articles, she focused on the poverty and hard living conditions she endured in the small southern towns she and her family lived in, but DeFuniak was never among the many towns she listed.

By the end of 1937, Jackie Cochran was a household name, and not just in the United States either. Named the Outstanding Woman Flier in the World the first of three times by the International League of Aviators, she also won her first Harmon trophy, which recognizes the nation's outstanding female pilot. She received the Harmon Trophy fifteen times in her life. She set several world speed records that year, and was the first woman pilot to make a blind landing, using only instruments.

We left California in late 1935 and moved back to Marianna, Florida, about 40 miles east of DeFuniak Springs, I believe because Dad and Jackie disagreed over something. Mother did not allow any argument or ugly talk. She somehow enforced peace. Unpleasantries and negatives may be a part of real life, but they just weren't discussed around us as children. My brother, Gordon, remembers some kind of difficulty between Jackie and Dad. My father could be as stubborn as Aunt Jackie and they certainly did not agree on everything.

It is plausible we left because Dad would not have gone along with any kind of secrecy. I know we were never 'pushed in the closet' when company came to the ranch, which was often, so how was our presence explained? How did she introduce us? Her public image included her story of being an orphan, but I can't see my father sitting still for anything other than her acknowledging us as her real family.

When Father, Mother and my siblings left California that December, we first went to my grandparents, my mother's parents' farm in Pansey, Alabama. Within weeks we settled in Marianna, Florida. Dad liked the town. He knew people there and he knew he could get work. We rented a house for a few months until my dad bought a home on five acres on the west side of town.

We were doing okay, but as Gordon said, "Back in those days, providing for eight people plus was not always easy. Daddy thought if we had a place where we could have a garden and grow a little extra to sell, it would help. It did.

"Things were pretty tough financially in those days," Gordon said. "There was not a lazy bone in our father's body, but there just was not always much work for a builder. He did the best he could. When things got really tough, Mother, whom Jackie loved dearly, would write to her and in a little while, a check would arrive in the mail. I know because I rode my bicycle to town to check the mail for that specific purpose. I don't think Daddy knew all about those times."

My parents also picked Marianna because it was near Mother's family just across the state line. My Grandpa

Ingram would occasionally walk the 25 miles from his farm in Pansey to Marianna to see us. Then he would walk 30 miles farther to Panama City, to visit his brother. He had a reputation as a great walker, and he preferred to use his own two feet to get him somewhere. I already adored him and thought this feat was quite phenomenal.

Aunt Jackie and Dad must have patched things up because she did come to see us after we left. In 1938 she flew into Tallahassee, rented a car to drive to Marianna. She talked anxiously about her plans for the next Bendix race. Even though we were just children, we understood our Aunt Jackie was trying to accomplish a lot of things.

Jackie won the Bendix Air Race that year and she also received the prestigious General William E. Mitchell Memorial Plaque for making the greatest contribution to aviation. She raced on setting records and by 1941 was one of the most famous aviatrix in the country.

On that trip in 1938 to Marianna she brought an envelope she asked Mother to keep for her but she did not tell Mother what was in it. She asked her not to open it except in the event of her death. Mother kept it in the bottom of her chifforobe. As children, we were naturally curious about the mystery package and asked Mother about it, but she just told us to not to touch it. We guessed it was Jackie's divorce papers from Robert Cochran, but we never really knew. After Mother died, we found the envelope when we were sorting through her belongings. Gordon called Aunt Jackie and asked what she wanted us to do with it. Jackie asked him to send it to her registered mail. He did. Of course, we really would have liked to have seen the contents since we had always been curious about the envelope, but we wouldn't have dared open it. It would have been a breach of Mother and Jackie's trust.

Billie Pittman Ayers and Beth Dees

It was on this same visit to Marianna in 1938 she had an intense conversation with Mother that has stayed in my mind over the years, even though I didn't understand it at the time. Gordon remembers it and my sister Bennie Rae, who has since died, was there, too. I guess we remembered it because we knew it was important even if we didn't know exactly what they were talking about. Aunt Jackie told my mother, "Ethel, you know I would give anything to trade places with you. You have so much.... the love in your family, a good life, these kids ..." she stopped talking because she was too upset. Then she said, "If I am ever found out, I swear I will go up in my plane and never return."

Just about anyone in America, except Mother, would have found Jackie's statement impossible to believe. Aunt Jackie had it all; fame, riches, beauty, brains. She had done very well for herself in the past few years. But looking back, I believe there was a shadow from past memories and untold truths that no amount of limelight could dispel. My mother did not argue with Aunt Jackie. We stayed quiet, knowing this was adult talk but later Bennie Rae and I did ask Mother why Aunt Jackie was sad. We were too young for details and she told us our aunt was upset about "some things that had happened." It really wasn't an answer, but we went on our way.

My mother loved Jackie dearly, as much as one of her own children. Jackie could have done anything and I know Mother would have said, "That's okay Jackie. I'm sure you did your best." And then she would have forgiven her. My mother understood how much Jackie wanted to put the past with its problems behind her. Both of my parents shared the burden of the secrets Aunt Jackie carried and they helped her through the hard times of her first failed marriage and

SUPERWOMAN Jacqueline Cochran

the death of her child. Mother, in particular, knew Grandmother to be domineering and demanding—not an easy mother for anyone to have. Yet, Mother also knew Jackie truly loved her mother anyway. This love was evident in the letters Jackie wrote to my grandmother and in all the many ways she helped my dad care for Grandmother in her later life.

It was not until we were grown and after Mother had passed away, we began to understood more about that adult conversation in the kitchen. It has become an important piece of the puzzle we have tried to put together in coming to terms with why Aunt Jackie's reinvented her early life story.

Dad may not have always agreed with his baby sister, but he always protected her. One Sunday afternoon Daddy answered the phone and a reporter with *Sports Illustrated Magazine* was on the line. He must have really done his homework because he had figured out we were Jackie's real family. Daddy listened for a few minutes—I could see he was getting angry—then, in no uncertain terms, he told the reporter, "When I have something to tell you about Jackie I'll call you," and he hung up. My sister said the reporter offered a large amount of money for the interview. But there was no decision to make. Dad was not interested in hiding anything but; he would not publicly refute Jackie's stories because he knew it would hurt her. It was very simple.

Chapter Nine: Jackie, Amelia Earhart and ESP

Grandmother wrote May 11, 1906, beneath Jackie's original name—Bessie Lee Pittman—on the paper kept in her Bible that was later given to me. May 11, 1906, matches the Pittman family information in the 1910 U.S. census. May 11, 1906 is the date of birth Bessie Pittman told the judge in her divorce proceedings in 1926. It is the same date Jackie Cochran gave on her passport application and on her first private pilot's license in 1932. Her birth date began fluctuating when the media attention began.

Question marks appear beside Jackie's year of birth in many biographical indexes, history books and other reference materials. She gave so many different dates during her lifetime; no one knew which one to use. I know its common for some women to subtract from their age a year or two, but it's somewhat amazing Jackie got away with straying up to 14 years from her real birth date. She usually, but not always got away with her discrepancy.

Probably, because she claimed to be an orphan, no one questioned the varying dates. But in a 1938 DeFuniak Springs newspaper article several residents took her to task for fudging on her age and other subjects. One woman said, "Bessie Pittman was a good looking girl, I'll say that for her, but if she's only 27 years old, I'll eat her beauty preparations, face creams, astringent lotions, freckle bleachers and all. She's ten years older than I am—if she's a day old and I'm —well, never mind how old I am, but I'm no spring chicken."

In 1964, the Federal Aviation Administration sent the 58-year-old pilot a form letter asking her to clarify the age discrepancies in her files before she could be issued her license renewal. She said she never received that letter. A second FAA form letter threatened to revoke Jackie's pilot's license if she failed to respond. Jackie fired back a three-page letter, indignant at being questioned. In detail, she explained she made herself older in her first years of flying so she could get her pilot's license because she didn't have parents to give her written permission, When she wrote the FAA apparently she forgot she had given her correct birth date on her first pilot license application. To my knowledge, there never have been age limits on earning a private pilot's license. Once FAA officials realized who she was, Jackie's letter quickly made its way up to the Chief of the Aero medical Division. A formal apology was extended, along with an invitation for her to visit their facilities. The request for further documentation was dropped. One internal department memo about the situation stated, "I get the feeling that her letter is as long as it is because she does feel somewhat embarrassed at having listed such widely varying birth dates."

As she grew older, Jackie grew more vague about her birth year, but she consistently throughout life considered May 11 an important date.

Jackie

"I don't know when I was born, but had chosen May 11 as a nice convenient date for the occasion. I figured that if an arbitrary date can be whipped up for the birthday of the queen of England, I could fix one for myself."

She always considered May 11 a special date, as she did the number '13'. On May 11 she married Floyd in 1936. She set several of her significant aviation records on May 11. Despite her no-nonsense personality and reliance on logic about most things in life, Aunt Jackie had a penchant for "special numbers." She had "13" painted on several of her racing planes.

Jackie did seem to have a special 'sense' about things. She claimed to have extrasensory perception. She believed most pilots had hunches, and felt hers were more pronounced than most. Over time she came to rely on this 'gift', as she strongly called it. She said she didn't expect anyone else to believe in this extra sensory power but Floyd did and so did her good friend Amelia Earhart.

Mutual friends introduced the two women at a dinner at their New York City home in 1935, although some say the two met earlier at an air race in New Bedford, Massachusetts. Amelia learned to fly a decade before Jackie and was already world famous for her solo flight across the North Atlantic two years earlier. Jackie said she knew within minutes of their first conversation at the dinner they would be good friends. "It was just one of the sure feelings you have occasionally when you meet a person," she said. Over lunch the next week, Amelia asked Jackie to fly with her on a weeklong trip to the west coast. The two grew close as they found many similar interests on such subjects as flying, religion, politics, science and their personal lives. Their differences, personality-wise, were as great as their similar interests. Floyd said of them, "They were two different characters, personalities, entirely. Amelia was quiet. Jackie was determined and forceful."

Along with their love of flying, they had something else in common—courage. Amelia spoke of it eloquently in her poem titled "Courage" which she wrote in 1927.

Courage is the price that Life exacts for granting peace,
The soul that knows it not, knows no release
From little things;
Knows not the mountain heights where bitter joy can hear
The sound of wings.

How can Life grant us boon of living, compensate
For dull gray ugliness and pregnant hate
Unless we dare
The soul's dominion? Each time we make a choice, we pay
With courage to behold resistless day
And count it fair.

The elite pilots of the day, such as Paul Mantz, Jimmy Doolittle and Roscoe Turner considered Cochran one of their own, while Amelia was thought of as quite daring, but quite average in her flying abilities. It took Amelia an unusually long time to learn to solo, while Jackie did in record time. Amelia appeared to other pilots uncertain about her flying abilities while Jackie had extraordinary confidence in what she could do.

Amelia laughed at some of their differences and said of Jackie, "Jackie Cochran loves to fly and loves to cook, but she doesn't like to service ships or do dishes". Jackie was aware of her "beloved friend's" shortcomings as a pilot but withheld her opinion until years after Amelia's death. She thought Amelia was a fair flyer, but considered her to be a

Billie Pittman Ayers and Beth Dees

lousy navigator. Still she believed in Amelia and her flying projects and helped finance several flights, including Amelia's ill-fated attempt to fly around the world.

Today, almost everyone recognizes the name of Amelia Earhart. There are too few who remember Jackie. Though it is well documented Jackie was by far the better pilot and contributed much more to aviation history, Amelia's mysterious disappearance over the Atlantic immortalized her.

Jackie considered Amelia such a close friend, that when Jackie was away on business, she allowed Amelia to stay in her bedroom, the only guest she extended this private courtesy to. In her dressing room, Jackie kept a treasured small silk American flag Amelia had carried on a special flight and autographed for her.

The California ranch became a second home to Amelia. It was very private. She and George spent her last Christmas at the Indio ranch. After she crashed in Hawaii on her first attempt to fly around the world Amelia asked Jackie if it would be all right if she came to stay at the ranch for a while. That first evening, Jackie said Amelia talked at length about the technical details of the accident, but Jackie felt Amelia was more shook up emotionally than she let on. Later, Jackie and Amelia studied and analyzed maps for a flight reversed from the original direction of the unsuccessful flight. Amelia spent about half of her last year at the ranch. She spent leisurely days swimming in the pool and horseback riding. On June 1, Jackie and Floyd met Amelia at the small airport near Miami to see Amelia off on her ill-fated flight.

Jackie disliked Amelia's husband, George, as much as she liked Amelia. Their relationship got off to a rocky start when George asked her in a patronizing manner, "Little girl, what do you want to do when you grow up?" She replied tartly, "Put your wife in the shade."

Jackie and Floyd thought George made a meal ticket off Amelia and that he was a 'lens louse' soaking up the publicity Amelia generated. Jackie wrote about one particularly telling incident about George in a magazine article for *The Ninety-Nines' Magazine*.

"I nearly threw George Putnam out of my ranch house one night I got so mad at him. He and Amelia had come down for a weekend after she had given a lecture in Pasadena. She was tired and I asked her if she would not like a bowl of milk toast. Her answer was an emphatic "yes." When I brought it in to her she was slouched a bit in a big, soft chair and started to sup the milk toast while in that position. George Putnam took her to task for slouching in the chair and said, 'If you want to be a lady you must act like a lady.' I told him he was out of place with such a criticism and he could not talk to her that way in my house." In another account of that incident, Jackie said she threw an ashtray at him.

Jackie

"If I should now refer to Amelia Earhart, practically everyone of you could tell me a lot about her, some of which would be almost pure fiction. Some of you would tell me that she was the one who flew that tri-motored Fokker across the Atlantic in 1928. She was only a passenger and, as she told me herself, for the sake of comfort she sat on the toilet seat most of the way across. The papers played her up big, called her the commander of the flight, which she wasn't, and gave her credit for its

success while (Wilmer) Stultz and (Louis) Gordon went into comparative oblivion.

"... Let no one think that in what I have just said I am attempting to talk down Amelia Earhart. Far from it. For this particular flight, she was dug out of her work with the children of foreign-born Americans at Denison Settlement in Boston. Mrs. Frederick Guest, a wealthy American born English woman by marriage had decided, following Charles Lindbergh's flight, to be the first woman to fly the Atlantic. She worked to that end with a group including George Putnam, an American publisher and writer. When, toward the end of the preparatory program, she either backed out or was talked out of making the flight, George Putnam got Amelia Earhart as a substitute. He needed her or some other woman for the publicity. Amelia had learned to fly about ten years earlier, but for financial and other reasons she had practically given up flying.

"No one knew more than Amelia how undeserved her fame was for that passenger flight with Stultz and Gordon. But it brought her the means and the connections, including George Putnam whom she married in 1931, to start out to justify her fame, and she did so in a big way. In 1932 she flew the Atlantic solo from New Foundland to Ireland in her Lockheed Monoplane, being the first woman to do so. Thereafter until her death in the Pacific in 1937, she reigned supreme among women flyers.

"Amelia organized the club of women flyers known as the "Ninety-Nines' Club", and in 1932 asked me to join. Later during the World War II years, I had the honor to be president of that club for two successive terms.

SUPERWOMAN Jacqueline Cochran

"...During the last year of her life, I was closer to Amelia Earhart than anyone else including, I believe, her own husband George Putnam. She stayed with me at the ranch ...for weeks before the start of her round-the-world flight, which ended in a take-off crash in Hawaii; and again she stayed with me while her plane was being repaired for her reverse direction flight, which ended in tragedy. My husband paid half the cost of repair of her plane. I knew her plans. We talked hours on end. I was fearful of results when change in direction of the flight was made. I got her to change navigators. When she left, she took with her in her plane a jackknife, fishing hooks and lines and a bright colored kite that I carried with me during my London to Australia race in 1934 against the possibility that I would get down in sea or in jungle.

"Amelia's accomplishments were many during the last nine years of her life. They included transcontinental record flights, a flight to and from Mexico City and a flight to the mainland from Honolulu. They were important in their day and kept her top place in aviation. But that's not what caused her memory to remain so vivid.

"...The memory of Amelia Earhart remains so vivid because she went down in a transpacific flight from Lae, New Guinea, to the Hawaiian Islands with a scheduled stop for refueling at Howland Island, a little beyond the half way point. Because the Government had built a runway for her use on tiny little Howland and a Coast Guard Cutter was stationed there for her arrival; because the Navy had a ship stationed halfway between Lae and Howland and another half way between Howland and Hawaii, because the Navy with ships and planes turned on a full scale search for her and her navigator Fred

Noonan that lasted several days; and because there was so much confusion about radio messages received and sent, and so much front page publicity about the flight right up to its tragic end, the whole thing developed into a mystery which has carried on through the years.

"Because a war with Japan was in the offing and Japan had a large group of mandated islands west and northwest of Howland, it was easy to think that Amelia and Noonan were on a spy mission for our Government. One of the moving picture companies played up this angle in a feature picture.

"...At this point I will only say that if Amelia was on a spy mission to make an air reconnaissance of the Truk area, our Government badly bungled the whole deal. Information is useless unless you receive it. To receive it at Howland, a tiny spot in the ocean, rather than at Lae was taking the extremely hazardous long shot when it was not necessary. It was no longer from Howland to Truk to Lae than from Lae to Truk to Howland, but one could hardly miss New Guinea, even with winds and dead reckoning. Without everything working in your favor, finding Howland would be like looking for a needle in a haystack. Amelia had at least 4,000 miles of range. She could have taken off from Honolulu and flown to Howland and back again failing to find it. But she had not such a safety factor on a 2,500-mile flight from Lae to Howland. She decided on the reverse direction flight while spending much time at our ranch while her plane was being repaired. I questioned the advisability of this change at the time. I don't think it was the result of Amelia's own judgment. I had an impression then, which I still hold, that it was George Putnam's doings for publicity purposes. Amelia, in fact, had some question the

flight should be abandoned altogether after the crash in Hawaii. One day at the ranch, my husband and Amelia got stuck in the desert sand in an old car and while waiting to be dug out, Amelia asked Floyd whether he thought she should continue the flight. He replied that if she was doing it to keep her place at the top among women in aviation, she was wasting her time and taking a big risk for nothing, because nothing and no one would topple her from the pinnacle, but if she were doing it for the adventure and just because she wanted to, no once could advise her against it because no one could decide such a thing for her."

Jackie and Amelia shared an avid interest in psychic phenomena and telepathic communications. The subject came up in their first trip west together. Jackie referred to it as "thought transmission." Amelia was impressed with Jackie's "thought transmissions". Hoping it would help in an emergency, they experimented with it for about a year before Amelia's last flight. Amelia would make flights, then check back to see how much Jackie knew about where she had been and when. Evidently they both felt Jackie was on target most of the time. Jackie was even 'aware' of a cabin fire Amelia had on the first leg of her flight from Burbank to Miami—in Amelia's first around-the-world flight attempt. But it was all for naught.

Jackie

"It was on the afternoon of July 2nd (of Amelia's last flight) that I came into the situation. But before telling you about this, I must give a preface in order not to be misunderstood.

"I don't believe in mediums or communications with the dear departed. I have never attended a séance in my life. I consider them pure bunk. My husband had been interested in years in what was known as psychic phenomenon. He did not believe in mediums either, but he, as a member of a committee, checked some on behalf of the Scientific American Magazine and otherwise, I would have no part of it. If God wants us to communicate with the dead he would not pick a medium to do the job for pay. But I had always had a strong sixth sense and rather successfully played my hunches. One night in about 1935, we attended a dinner party in New York and a man was there who was working on extra sensory perception for Duke University. He had some of his test cards along and wanted to try us out, presumably for entertainment. The cards, five in number, each with a different figure on its face were placed face down on a table behind a screen, and as the man lifted one at a time, I was to guess what card was lifted. I guessed them all correctly which, to the man, was astounding. Later, Dr. Rhine of the Parapsychology Department of Duke University wanted to work with me but I refused. My husband was equally astounded over this 100% accuracy at guessing the cards. The next morning, with my eyes closed, he held his fingers, with changes in number; behind my head and in each I told him correctly how many he was holding up. So then he began working with me fairly regularly. I could read letters before they had arrived. I told him in New York about the sudden death of one of his associates in San Francisco several hours before he received the news. I called him in New York at midnight once and told him exactly what he had been doing from dinnertime on, and what I said he confirmed

as correct in all particulars. I even developed the knack of doing automatic writing. I would in this way tell of things going on around the world, but it always concerned the living, not the dead. I would become emotionally exhausted after each such experience but carried on for Floyd's sake because he thought I was delineating some new perimeters of the human mind.

"It was during this period that Amelia Earhart came closely into my life. She, too, was very interested in extrasensory perception and had studied all that Duke University had to offer on the subject at the time. She was intrigued by my apparent capacity when called upon to tell what was going on at a distance. One night at the ranch, the radio told of a transport plane disappearing en route to Salt Lake City. She asked me to try and locate it. I did, with names of mountains and roads and even the location of power lines and a pile of telephone poles. Neither of us knew the area, which was in the mountains north and east of Salt Lake City, but she called Paul Mantz in Los Angeles. He got out a map of the area and confirmed all my descriptions. Amelia was so impressed that she drove into Los Angeles that night and took off for Salt Lake City the next morning. She conducted an air search of the area without results. But the plane was found next spring after the snow had melted, right where I said it was. A little later, another plane failed to show up at its destination in Los Angeles. Amelia called me on the phone from Los Angeles and I told her where the plane was on a mountainside not far out of Los Angeles. I told her how many were killed and how many injured, and that some were already making their way down the mountain. She located it just where I said it would be and got the credit for being quite a seer. All this convinced

Amelia that if she were to get down on her round-the-word flight, I could locate her. We tried it on one of her trips across the continent.

"...George Putnam knew about most of these tests. As soon as she heard that Amelia had not reached Howland Island, he called me on the phone and came over to my apartment. We were both in Los Angeles at the time. This is what I told him as best I can remember. I wrote it down but tried unsuccessfully to find that writing among my files.

"Amelia out of fuel, landed in the ocean northwest of Howland and not too far away. The plane is floating. Amelia is not hurt, but Fred Noonan bumped against the bulkhead during the water landing and is unconscious with an injured head. There is an American boat called the Itasca in the vicinity...

"I can't remember the name of the Japanese fishing boat, but I think it was something like Maru or Mari. I had never heard of the Itasca at the time. The next day I told George Putnam the plane was still afloat and drifting eastward north of Howland. The next day I told George it was too late to rescue Amelia. I was very sad and also very disgusted that I had not been able to be more precise and of help. I went to the cathedral and said a prayer for Amelia and lit candles for her. From that moment until now, I have never tried out my so-called extra-sensory perception. It did not rescue Amelia and I did most of the work against that possibility.

"As for George Putnam, I never saw him again after that meeting on July 2, 1937 in my Los Angeles apartment. I resented him because I thought he pushed Amelia into this trip for moneymaking purposes. Amelia could not write her contemplated book. But Putnam did—

called My Last Flight. He dedicated it to "Floyd" and went on to other marriages and money making schemes until death caught up with him and of all places, he came down with his final illness in Death Valley."

During the early 1960s, Jackie corresponded with at least four "mediums" or psychics regarding questions about Amelia. None of their answers satisfied her curiosity. In a letter to one psychic in Dallas, Jackie wrote, "I recognize that extra-sensory perception presents a great field of research and possible development. At one time I also did some automatic writing. I worked quite a bit with Amelia along these lines, all as generally stated in my book. I am satisfied of the reality of thought transmission between living persons. I am not convinced that the so-called messages from the departed are more than such thought transmissions between the living and the operation of one's own subconscious mind. I have not personally attempted any work in ESP since the days of Amelia."

To test this psychic, Jackie asked her a series of questions about where she had been on a certain day, when did she meet Amelia, what item of Amelia's did she keep in her dressing room, etc. Several months after receiving the psychic's response, Jackie wrote her a terse letter back saying none of her answers were right.

Another outstanding woman pilot, Beryl Markham, was staying at the Indio ranch when Amelia disappeared in July 1937. She was waiting to meet Amelia when she finished her flight. Raised by her English father in Africa, Beryl became a bush pilot and the year she visited Jackie had become world famous for being the first person to fly solo across the Atlantic the hard way—against the headwinds—from England to North America. In her memoirs later,

Beryl recounted how Jackie's house was swamped with reporters after Amelia disappeared. The media had found out about the psychic pact between the Amelia and Jackie.

Because of their close friendship, Jackie delivered several eulogies for Amelia. She told a crowd of several hundred gathered at one sponsored by The New York City branch of the Women's International Associations of Aeronautics, "if her last flight was into eternity one can mourn her loss, but not regret her effort."

Both women had been active in the Ninety-Nines' Club. Amelia had helped organize the international group of women pilots in 1929 and served as the first president. Twenty-six licensed women pilots first met informally in Cleveland after participating in the "Powder Puff Derby", a women's race that opened the National Air Race. Amelia had encouraged Jackie to join. Jackie later led the group as president from 1941 to 1943.

SUPERWOMAN Jacqueline Cochran

Amelia Earhart (left) often stayed at the Odlum-Cochran ranch because of the privacy offered. Despite different personalities,, their interest in subjects like flying and even ESP kept Amelia's and Jackie's friendship close.

Billie Pittman Ayers and Beth Dees

Chapter Ten: Queen WASP in WWII

Of the 675 women pilots licensed to fly when WWII began, some wanted to use their flying skills to defend their country. Bringing women into the military to fight in combat was not a revolutionary idea world-wise, but America wasn't ready for it then and still struggles with related issues today. Jackie tried to help. In *The New York Tribune*, in her usual terse style, she wrote about women's efforts in earlier wars. She wrote about how Ruth Law, an aviatrix who had set aviation records and won races, tried unsuccessfully to join the air forces in America when World War I began, then went to France, where she was also rejected. Jackie told about how another aviatrix, Katherine Stinson, and her sister, Marjorie, operated a flying school to train Canadian pilots. Their brother was the then-famous pilot, Eddie Stinson who taught American cadets to fly. She described how females acted as saboteurs in the American Revolution.

Jackie knew she knew she could fly a plane as well as any man and knew other women could too. Two years before WWII, she talked in person with First Lady Eleanor Roosevelt about preparing a group of woman pilots to help with the war efforts. In 1939 when Eleanor wrote Jackie congratulating her on being the first woman pilot to make a blind landing, using the plane's instruments only, Jackie seized the opportunity and wrote back, jumping to her point in the letter's second paragraph.

Jackie

"I am taking advantage of this opportunity to lay before you a thought which I hope will commend itself to you.

"Should there be a call to arms it is not my thought that women pilots will go out and engage in combat, for I'm sure they won't. But every trained male pilot will be needed in active service. The "lady birds" could do all sorts of helpful work back of the men's work. Every woman pilot who can step into the cockpit of an ambulance plane, or courier plane, or commercial or transport plane can release a male pilot for more important duty."

She made sure the First Lady knew that Germany, Russia, England and France had already started programs for training women pilots. Convinced Jackie's ideas had true merit, the First Lady replied:

"Dear Miss Cochrane (sic):

Thank you for your letter of September 28. Your suggestion is good and I think it is a necessary development. I will bring it to the attention of the Army, Navy and the Coast Guard."

With a letter of support from President Roosevelt, Jackie approached her good friend General H. "Hap" Arnold, the Chief of the Air Corps and proposed the training program for women pilots. She explained how women pilots could take care of ferrying responsibilities, and free up male pilots to fly combat. He listened, but was not convinced. He put her off.

A few months later Jackie carefully handpicked a group of 25 of America's top women pilots to go to England to work as volunteers with the Royal Air Force. Ann Wood-Kelly was among those she chose and they remained friends for life. Ann said Jackie was "the most remarkable woman I've known" and remembered how Jackie would check on the girls every day to make sure they were comfortable and had what they needed. They ferried planes for the British Air Transport Auxiliary (ATA), which already was using women pilots. Partly to inspire public confidence that women could fly military planes, in 1941 Jackie, flew a Hudson bomber to England in a highly publicized event.

Jackie

"This flight [Hudson Bay Bomber Flight] really got started when Clayton Knight and I dined with General "Hap" Arnold ... Knight was trying to get pilots to fly for the British Ferry Command, delivering planes across the North Atlantic, and General Arnold, being much interested in helping the British, asked me if I could help Knight. He then added, 'Why don't you fly some planes across, yourself. It would be helpful all around.'

I needed nothing more to set me off, because I wanted very much to get into the war effort activity and to get to England where the Battle of Britain was fast building up. ...On delivery of the plane in Prestwick, (Scotland) I went by train to London where I spent several days. First of all I went out and called on Lord Beaverbrook. He was curious whether I had brought any fresh oranges or lemons along, and I succeeded in trading two lemons for a cartoon of himself which he had hanging on his wall. He had the cartoon delivered, and the lemons picked up by armored car."

...I also went to see Pauline Gower, to find out how she was handling the women pilots who were working for the flying forces of England, because I felt we might need to do something like that at home soon."

Exhausted but back on American soil Jackie went to bed saying she was not to be disturbed. But she was disturbed by a telegram from the White House inviting her to lunch that day with President Roosevelt. After lunch, they spent the afternoon in his library discussing the war situation in England and at home.

Jackie was placed in charge of organizing the Women Air Service Pilots, called the WASP. Meticulous screening of about 25,000 applicants produced an elite group of 1,830 women to go through the WASP training program. Jackie paid for the custom designed silver wings pilot pin pinned on each woman pilot graduating in the first class. 1,074 women pilots made it through the program to take their place as trainees in the Army Air Corps.

"These women ferried aircraft from factory to the airfields or wherever they were needed. They tested planes that had been damaged in battle and repaired. They taught men to be pilots. They towed targets behind them in their planes for the ground troops to practice shooting. They flew tracking and searchlight missions, and test piloted planes. Between 1943 and 1944 the WASP covered some millions of air miles flying 77 different types of aircraft—nearly every plane the Army had in its inventory—fighters, transports, cargo and bombers. A couple of WASP was certified to fly the huge Boeing B-29 Super fortress.

The first class of WASP trained at Howard Hughes Municipal Airport in Houston, Texas but the training facilities were later moved to Avenger field at Sweetwater,

Texas. Although they were not officially part of the military, and not bound by its laws, the women lived as soldiers; living in barracks, eating in mess halls, training physically and mentally to fly, and observing strict military codes of conduct. It was jokingly referred to as 'Cochran's Convent,' because Jackie expected the women to live as soldiers, act like ladies and devote themselves to the cause of winning the war.

The WASP helped America win WWII and represented a major breakthrough in advancing women in society.

Jackie

"The first class started at Houston, Texas, with as motley a group of flying equipment as one can imagine and with the trainees housed in motor courts. We finally moved to Avenger Field, Sweetwater, Texas, which was given by the Air Force Cadet Training Command for our use. There the trainees slept six to a bay and while civilian in status the operation was conducted on a military basis. We had more than 200 standard type training planes. The girls could resign at any time or they could be eliminated for cause, but only after charges and a hearing and findings. …. We have very minimal disciplinary work to do. Avenger Field was known as Cochran Convent. The trainees were somewhat awed by me and somewhat scared of me. There were no scandals and that seems to be true of the girls throughout life. They were well trained and well chosen. The women pilot program was very experimental at the start and without the stabilizing effect of militarization. Any little thing could have knocked it off track ... The women and the (male) cadets received the same training.

"They (WASP) were an accomplishment. They had flown 60 million miles on operational missions. They have flown every type of equipment including the B-26 and the B-17. They had performed every type of non-combat duty including simulated strafing, smoke laying, radio control flying, target towing and engineering test flying besides ferrying. They put in as many hours per month as the male pilots on similar work. Their accident rate and fatalities were as low as in the case of the male pilots. The heads of several commands to which the WASP were assigned thought they did better than the men, particularly in some of the flying chores that were considered monotonous, such as target towing."

This is an excerpt from her lengthy, detailed official report on the WASP at the war's end.

1. "That women meeting the proper height and weight standards could be trained as quickly and as economically as men in the same group to fly all types of planes safely, efficiently and regularly; and that physiology peculiar to women is not a handicap to dependable performance of duty in a properly selected group.
2. "That an effective women's air force of many scores of thousands of good dependable pilots could be built up in case of need from the women of our country between the ages of 18 and 28."

Later in a report summary in *Education Magazine*, as a vice-president for the National Aeronautics Association she wrote, "Both the accident rate and the fatality rate compared favorably with the rates for male pilots doing similar work."

She requested military status for the WASP, 38 of which lost their lives in the service for their country. It was denied. Because they lacked official military status, those WASP who died in training accidents received no death, burial benefits, special compensation or military honors as did their male counterparts. In several cases the women in training simply 'passed the hat' to take up money to help pay the costs of sending the bodies home.

Despite initial doubt about having women in the military, after seeing their competency first-hand during the war, General Arnold fully supported WASP militarization. "The WASP proved they could fly wing tip to wing tip with their brothers," he said. In addressing the last graduating class he said, "We will not look again upon a woman flying organization as experimental—a pioneering venture, yes—solely an experiment, no. The WASP's are an accomplishment.

But male pilots with the Civil Aeronautics who felt they had more flight experience than the WASP and were facing unemployment with the war's end approaching strongly resisted. They feared the women pilots would get their jobs.

Jackie

"The reason for the creation of the WASP in 1942 was fast disappearing in the fall of 1944 when the tide of war had turned our way. Manpower would be returning home and the male pilots would not like to be idle while the WASP were piling up hours in the air. General Arnold and I were in agreement that the

SUPERWOMAN Jacqueline Cochran

WASP should be disbanded and with two months prior notice the deactivation occurred December 7, 1944."

Each pilot received a telegram from the Army Air Force thanking him or her for their patriotic contributions, but stating their services were no longer needed. Jackie also sent each a telegram again thanking them and trying to ease what for most of the WASP felt was like a terrible, demoralizing blow. The last class graduated Dec. 7, 1944.

Four years later women were granted permanent status in the armed forces and the Air Force allowed WASP veterans to join the Air Force Reserve but, it wasn't until 1977, when the G.I. Improvement Act and Public Law 95-202 was signed, that the WASP's contributions were acknowledged as "active military service."

When they were officially enlisted in 1977, the 900 remaining WASP became military veterans, entitled to benefits. However, they did not receive the same benefits as the WWII male veterans. There were no G.I. educational benefits, national service life insurance, farm or home loan provisions. In 1984, the WASP still alive were given the "World War II Victory Medal" and the "American Theater Medal" which their male co-patriots had been awarded right after WWII.

Thankfully in October 1997, honor and attention was focused on the 1.8 million women who have served in the U.S. Military with the unveiling of the new Women in the Military Service for America Memorial, which was dedicated in Arlington, Virginia. Also the 50th anniversary of WWII has brought more emphasis on the contributions WASP and other women made to the war effort.

It was General Hap Arnold's son, Bruce, who rose to a colonel, who championed the WASP's cause through the years. U.S. Senator Barry Goldwater was also a strong advocate and lobbyist, as was Lindy Boggs of Louisiana who introduced the bill.

Jackie's voice was constantly raised in support. In 1951 she held a posh reunion for the WASP at her ranch. Throughout the years the group has held many annual gatherings. Jackie was the guest of honor at a 1964 WASP gathering held in Cincinnati. That same year in May and June Jackie flew a Lockheed 104 jet "Starfighter" to set several international speed records. Jackie also gathered with the WASP in 1972 when they met in Sweetwater, Texas.

Jackie

"I don't know what is the single outstanding service I had given my country. But I think most people would say it was the organizing and directing of the Women Air Force Pilots during the war period. They were known as WASP. It was among my outstanding accomplishments, at least it was what I got my Distinguished Service Medal for with the citation by President Roosevelt and the presentation by General Henry "Hap" Arnold, while at least 20 general officers stood at attention."

Even when she was busiest of times, traveling constantly with many responsibilities, Jackie remembered family. In 1945 I was living in New England with my husband, Mose, who was away with his squadron and came home to Marianna for the birth of Linda, our oldest daughter. I remember Aunt Jackie getting together with Mother and Aunt Elvie in Mobile where Aunt Elvie still

SUPERWOMAN Jacqueline Cochran

lived. They just wanted to visit. Jackie stayed in touch with Mother until her death in 1970.

Despite the breakup of the WASP, Jackie managed to keep herself where the action was. It was during the war days the military came out with its first jet—the Bell P-59—and Jackie managed to get a ride in it. She was the first woman to fly a jet. Her first flight was at the controls of a GF 33 trainer. She loved the jets most likely because like her, they were known for their power, efficiency and speed.

Ostensibly as a correspondent for *Liberty Magazine*, which Floyd owned, Jackie was one of only two women—the other was a major news correspondent—aboard the U.S.S. Missouri in the Philippines in 1945 to watch Japanese General Yamashita sign surrender papers at the end of WWII. Jackie confessed she almost got ahead of herself when she flew on to Japan, arriving there even before General McArthur's official visit. Later, while traveling in China, she was invited to lunch with Madame Chiang Kai-shek and several days later met with the Communist leader Mao Tse-tung. She attended the Nuremberg War Crime Trials and later in Berlin she wrangled her way inside the underground living quarters of Adolf Hitler. She managed this by trading a couple of packs of cigarettes to a guard in exchange for the chance to look in the place where the man who gave orders to end so many lives finally ended his own.

Because of her work with the WASP, in 1945 Jackie became the first women civilian to be awarded the U.S. Distinguished Service Medal. Jackie's patriotism was strong and resolute. Floyd felt the same. During the war they saw little of each other as they went in different directions, turning their time and energies into doing what they could for their country. Floyd was paid $1 a year for his work for presidents Hoover, Roosevelt and Truman. He directed the office of Production Management during WWII and later he pushed for the development of the Atlas Missile. He so believed in the project that started man on his way to the moon that when the U.S. Government cut back on funding the Atlas missile in the 50's, Floyd kept the project alive with his own corporate funds until the government renewed its interest several years later. He paid for the first Atlas missile out of his own pocket.

Other countries honored Jackie for her help during the war and for her accomplishments in aviation. In 1949 Jackie was awarded the French Legion of Honor, also collected air medals from Belgium, Spain, Thailand, Turkey and Rumania.

Jackie's active duty station in the Office of Legislative Liaison after WWII gave her the unique opportunity to continue her patriotic duty and meet some of the most important people in the country.

Politically adept and cause-oriented, Jackie made tremendous breakthroughs for women, but she avoided identifying with women's rights groups and did not consider herself a feminist. Whereas Amelia Earhart, until her death, championed women's rights and civil rights, often speaking at rallies and throwing the weight of her fame into causes, Jackie didn't. She scoffed at the early Women's Liberation movement. "Liberation from what?" she was quoted as saying. She was outspoken and assertive, not particularly common attributes for the average housewife at that point in history. She worked easily and efficiently within the upper echelons of a male-dominated power structure. Once described as "an iron fist in a velvet glove," Jackie mastered the art of charm, but could be as belligerent as the most macho male. Her complex approach appeared contradictory at times. She wasn't out to outdo men, but she made sure her gender didn't get in the way of her doing what she wanted.

A *New York Times* article in May of 1940 read, "Aviatrix Sees Advance in Woman's Cause Paid For in Loss of Homage to Femininity" in which Jackie cautioned that women might be winning their social and political independence at the sacrifice of the old-fashioned homage to femininity enjoyed by their grandmothers.

"We're carrying the idea of parity too far. It's getting so a woman just about has to do a headstand on Forty-second Street to receive any attention. There was a time when it was quite a thing just to be a woman."

The same month an article appeared in a business and professional women's magazine where she talked about equality and, at times, the superiority of women. "I found no differences between the efficiency quotient for men and women, and oftentimes I have found that women have many more desirable traits. Among them is a more sensitive, intuitive sense of training and handling personnel, more stick-to-itiveness on details and important follow through; many times they are more imaginative, practical and thoughtful," she said.

In 1947 Jackie was asked to serve on a special committee led by Senator Stuart Symington, who had been Secretary of Air during WWII. The committee drew up legislative proposals to make the air forces a separate branch of the armed forces. They also addressed what part women should play in the new United States Air Force.

It seems contradictory Jackie did so much through her accomplishments to advance women's rights, but voted against their advancement in the military and later, in the space program. Through her own WASP experience Jackie knew women pilots were as competent as the men, but as a member of Symington's committee she came out adamantly opposed to the idea of making females part of the regular Air Force. Asked if women should be put on equal flying status with the men, Jackie said "No."

Jackie

"When the legislation was being prepared, I was asked to give my recommendations as to whether women should be on flying status...I recommended from an economic status that women not be put on flying status." She explained her position by saying the high cost to the government to train a pilot would be an economic disaster if that pilot was a woman who decided to marry and stay home to raise a family. *"I strongly recommended, and it was carried of course, that women not be put on flying status, for that reason."*

It took nearly another half century before 1st Lieutenant Kelly Flinn, in 1993, became the first to train and graduate as the first female combat pilot for a B-52 bomber.

Later as a special consultant to the National Aeronautics and Space Administration, she essentially took the same stand...that it was not a good value for the taxpayer to spend money to train a woman, who might not fulfill her duties because of involvement in family life. Although her vote on the Symington's committee passed without comment, her opposition to including women in the space program then did not go unnoticed. Word of her opposition got out and she set about defending herself. In a letter to one prominent columnist she wrote,

Jackie

"Please doesn't publicize me as against women in space. There are sure to be there as they were found in the balloons, gliders and powered aircraft. I only want them to get there in the right way, at the right time, so as to do credit to themselves and not to interfere with the current expensive and nationally important phase of space flight."

In a magazine article she wrote:

Jackie

"Our American Space program as a whole of which our manned flight project is a part, is exceedingly urgent in the national interest and also is terribly expensive to the taxpayer. Time is of the essence. The manned space flight program even in its primary stages makes money look like confetti. Every such flight runs into the millions. It costs hundreds of thousands of dollars to train a good fighter or bomber pilot. It costs even more to train an astronaut. The first manned space flights of the "Mercury Project" were simple compared with what must come in connection with the "Gemini Project" (rendezvous in space) and the "Apollo Project" (trip to the moon).

"Every national interest and all sound reasoning we start out with the most completely qualified candidates from who our few astronauts would be selected. The most qualified happened to be men—not because they were men, but for reasons I will state. If women had been selected in these early stages or even now, it would have been a clear case of discrimination against the men—like

the moving of women to the head of the line just because they were women.

"There are only a handful of women who would don the space suit and enter the capsule for a blast off even if given the opportunity. I know, because I tried to get a group of women pilots to take the preliminary medical test for those who passed might lead to further tests. It was pure medical research and not official in any way. But enough had taken these tests to reach valid findings as to the psychological and physiological capacities of women to stand the sudden extra forces of gravity (known as g's), the long period of weightlessness and the many other things a space flyer must experience and withstand. We have found out how women stack up compared with men in these respects. The fact is that only twenty women responded to the invitation for the free tests.

Twelve of the twenty passed which is about the same percentage as in the case of the men applicants. That did not mean that these women were ready for astronaut training. It could, however, have meant that somewhere along the way a training program for women for space flight might have evolved. Unfortunately, the research project was called off before the further laboratory tests were made because the authorities stated there was "no present need" for such test. That was of course true. But there was I believe a sound reason for these inexpensive experimental tests and I hope they will be put back on the tracks. The day will come as sure as I am writing these words when women will go into space in one capacity or another provided they are physically and emotionally equipped to do so, as I believe to be the case. The sooner we find out about these factors the better. One or two women cannot produce adequate proof. A group is necessary for this purpose. The twelve women pilots who passed these preliminary tests are naturally disappointed that more were not done with them. Most of them however, are realistic while hopeful."

In a lengthy detailed letter to Dr. Randall Lovelace, director of the clinic, which conducted many of the tests for the women in the space program, Jackie wrote:

Jackie

"As one who for about twenty five years has been claming and trying to prove that women are as good in aviation as men, I look with great favor on the program involving women in space. I wish that age were not a bar to my active participation in the group. I want them to succeed! They can, but starting with a very small group this will take a lot of doing, considering the normal attrition rates and life factors.

"...These thoughts are not new. I have had them since the Mercury program was started. I have expressed them before the subcommittee of Congress appointed to investigate the standards set by NASA for astronauts.

"One or two of the women who were crowding to get the Mercury program opened to women thought my attitude and my testimony indicated I was against women in space. Just the contrary was true. I want the path to the moon open to all. To try to crash the expensive gate to that path at the wrong time and in the wrong way would, in my opinion, only delay a successful entry supported by full credentials."

Jackie's active duty station in the Office of Legislative Liaison after World War II gave her the unique opportunity to continue her patriotic duty and meet some of the most important people in the country.

Politically adept and cause-oriented, Jackie made tremendous breakthroughs for women in many areas, but she avoided identifying with women's rights groups. She did not consider herself a feminist. Whereas Amelia Earhart, until her death, championed women's rights and civil rights, often speaking at rallies and throwing the weight of her fame into causes, Jackie didn't. She scoffed at the early Women's Liberation movement. "Liberation from what?" she was quoted as saying. She was outspoken and assertive, not particularly common attributes for the average housewife at that point in history. She worked easily and efficiently within the upper echelons of a male-dominated power structure. Once described as "an iron fist in a velvet glove," Jackie had mastered the art of charm, but could be as belligerent as the most macho male. Hers' was a complex approach that appeared contradictory at times. She wasn't out to outdo men, but she fought to keep her gender from being used against her pursuing her goals.

A *New York Times* article in May of 1940 read, "Aviatrix Sees Advance in Woman's Cause Paid For in Loss of Homage to Femininity" in which Jackie warned that women might be winning their social and political independence at the sacrifice of the old-fashioned homage to femininity enjoyed by their grandmothers.

Jackie

"We're carrying the idea of parity too far. It's getting so a woman just about has to do a headstand on Forty-

second Street to receive any attention. There was a time when it was quite a thing just to be a woman."

The same month an article appeared in a business and professional women's magazine where she talked about equality and, at times, the superiority of women.

Jackie

"I found no differences between the efficiency quotient for men and women, and oftentimes I have found that women have many more desirable traits. Among them is a more sensitive, intuitive sense of training and handling personnel, more stick-to-itiveness on details and important follow through; many times they are more imaginative, practical and thoughtful."

One might think Jackie would lead the way for women to be accepted into the astronaut program, but she actually testified before Congress in 1962 against their being introduced into the ongoing Mercury Astronaut Program. Although she states in numerous publications that "women will fly into space just as certainly as men" and "women can be just as good astronauts as men," she argued before a congressional committee it didn't make sense economically for the government to spend hundreds of thousands of dollars in training a female who might marry, become pregnant and want to raise children instead. This was the same reasoning she used against women being part of the Air Force in 1947, but this time her testimony was made public and became part of a clamor of controversy. She wrote a letter to one prominent columnist.

"Please don't publicize me as against women in space. They are sure to be there as they were found in the balloons, gliders and powered aircraft. I only want them to get there in the right way, at the right time, so as to do credit to themselves and not to interfere with the current expensive and nationally important phase of space flight."

Some columnists accused her of egotism, saying Jackie was jealous of any female who would fly into space and so steal her limelight. Others saw her as gutsy in speaking out candidly against the feminists of the day.

Jackie did say she would have given anything to be the first woman in space. She actually wanted to be the first person in space. Age-related health problems prevented her pursuit of these goals. Still, she made important contributions in opening that frontier. She was involved as early as 1959 when NASA set the criteria to select the first team of male astronauts. She was on the NASA board. At Mayo Clinic, she underwent tests similar to those the men went through at the Lovelace Foundation in Albuquerque, New Mexico. In 1960 and 1961 in follow-up tests she ran into a problem. While being spun in a centrifuge, she experienced pain in the middle of her shoulders, which usually indicated there was some impairment in the lungs or heart. It turned out to be a foretelling incident to her serious heart problems in the 1970s. Though women were denied being admitted into the astronaut program, a small group of women were selected to undergo tests to see how they would fare in space. As a show of support, Jackie helped pay—where needed—for the transportation and other costs for the women who took part in the tests. As a special consultant for NASA, she stayed closely involved in the fledgling program.

SUPERWOMAN Jacqueline Cochran

In 1983, Sally Kirsten Ride became the first American female astronaut to go into space in the space shuttle Challenger. A dozen years later Eileen Collins became the first female to pilot a space shuttle.

Billie Pittman Ayers and Beth Dees

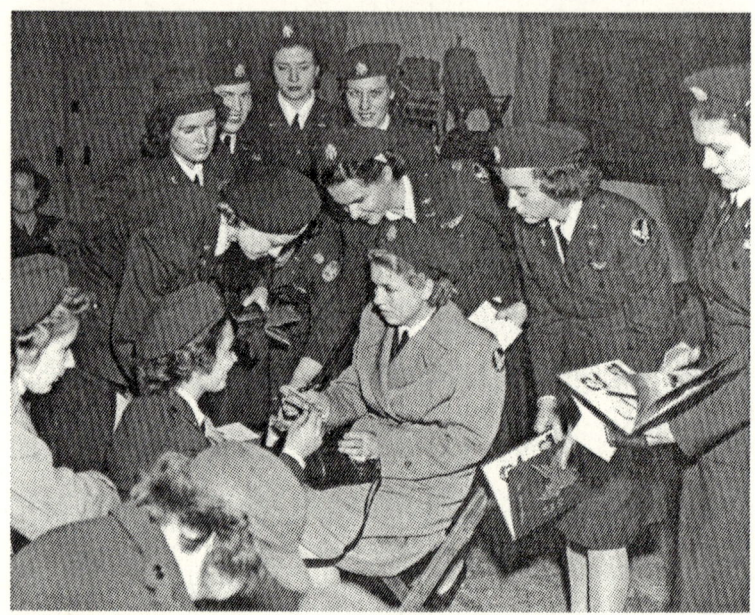

In this U.S. Army photo, graduating WASP trainees gather around Jackie to receive their silver wings and get WASP books autographed.

Chapter Eleven: Eisenhower and LBJ's Sunday Visit

Jackie influenced American history as well as aviation history. She is credited with the effort that convinced General Eisenhower to run for president. She also helped a seriously ill Lyndon Baines Johnson get emergency medical treatment during his Senate campaign in 1948.

Jackie was by nature political, always weighing the advantages and disadvantages, aware of who held the power, working to develop friendships and alliances, but she didn't get actively involved with national politics until the late 1940s. Before that, she and Floyd voted as Independents.

Jackie got a call one day from a key Republican Party leader asking her to help organize a rally at New York's Madison Square Garden to show support for Eisenhower. The rally would be taped and shown to Eisenhower to help convince him of the public support he would have if he ran for president. At this time Eisenhower was in Paris as the head of NATO. He said he would run for the presidency only if he got a "clear cut call from the people." The Republicans, with Jackie's help, set out to make this happen.

With Tex McCreary as her co-chairman, Jackie worked non-stop for months, phoning volunteers, flying to organizational meetings and booking the Garden. McCreary planned the program itself, putting together an exciting vaudeville show. Details were everything to Jackie. She called a well-known weather forecaster, Dr. Irving Krick, who had forecast the weather for the famous

D-Day invasion in WWII, to make sure the weather was going to be okay on February 8, the day of the event. It was.

To ensure there were enough people for the event, Jackie planned the political event to follow a big boxing match. The fight lasted until 11 p.m. The rally planners hoped some of the match observers would stay for the show. Most of them did and when the Eisenhower supporters arrived, as planned, it was wall -to -wall people. Approximately 35,000 people turned out, more than double what the Garden was designed to hold. The rally lasted until 5 a.m.

Jackie went home, collapsed into bed but within a few hours she got a phone call asking her to fly with Henry Cabot Lodge to France personally deliver the tape to Eisenhower. Running on adrenaline, she packed and left immediately on a commercial flight.

Eisenhower agreed to see the tape and set up an appointment. Mrs. Eisenhower and General Gruenther were among those who gathered for the viewing. Jackie said the general was moved to tears by the rough, uncut, unedited film of thousands of people yelling, "We want Ike." Jackie is given credit for coining the popular campaign slogan, "I like Ike". Afterwards General Eisenhower told Jackie he would run for the presidency and asked her to discretely contact several key people back in the states. Jackie followed through.

In his book ***Mandate for Change*** Eisenhower wrote, "Among my many visitors in the ensuing weeks were several who later became publicly active in the "Citizens for Eisenhower" groups, the at first informal organizations that never ceased their work until the climax later that year. Many were good friends; I could question neither their

SUPERWOMAN Jacqueline Cochran

dedication nor their integrity. Two days earlier there had been a mass meeting at midnight in New York's Madison Square Garden, arranged by supporters who were hoping by this means to add weight to their argument that I should become a candidate. The entire proceedings were put on film. As soon as the film was processed, Miss Cochran flew the Atlantic and brought it immediately to Paris. Her second task was to get me to sit still long enough to view it. By the time she reached our home she had gone thirty-five hours without sleep.

As we conferred, Miss Cochran told me about the opposition of the so-called 'pros' in politics, who although part of the Eisenhower groups, believed that no meeting of this kind, held after the completion of a Garden fight the same evening, could possibly draw a crowd at midnight. They felt that a poor turnout would slow up the "Eisenhower Movement" which they thought was then gaining momentum. Miss Cochran asked that my wife be with me when we viewed the film. It was shown in our living room at Villa St. Pierre in Manes-la-Coquette.

... It was a moving experience to witness the various unanimity of such a huge crowd [in Madison Square Garden]—to relate that everyone present was enthusiastically supporting me for the highest office of the land. As the film went on, Mamie and I were profoundly affected. The incident impressed more than had all the arguments present by the individuals who had been plaguing me with political questions for many months. When our guests departed, I think we both suspected, although we did not say so, that our lives were to be once more uprooted.

After Jacqueline Cochran's visit I had talked with General Lucius Clay of February 16, 1952. He flew to

London, at the time of King George VI's death and asked me to meet with him at the London home of Brigadier Sir James Gault, my British military assistant in WWII. George Allen and Sid Richardson, two friends from the States were also there. At this meeting I tentatively agreed that I would return home to the United States as soon as I could complete my duties in Europe, and if nominated at the convention, would campaign for the presidency. I was committed in my own mind to run if nominated, but not to seek the nomination."

Later, Jackie flew around the country making several hundred speeches whipping up support for Eisenhower. She met with Walt and Roy Disney, the business manager, to ask Disney to create an animated film for the Eisenhower campaign. Again, she had the necessary connections. Not only was Floyd on the board of Disney corporation, Roy was a frequent guest at their ranch. He also was a staunch Republican. Several dozen of Disney's employees volunteered to help and the cartoon enjoyed widespread play on television stations across the country. Eisenhower won by a wide margin.

After Eisenhower was elected, Jackie and Floyd stayed in close contact and their friendship grew. Jackie and Floyd were invited to many state dinners and functions with the president and on one occasion in 1957 Jackie was asked to represent the president as a special ambassador at the Inauguration of President Somoza in Managua.

The Eisenhowers were drawn, as were others, to the quiet privacy provided at the Cochran-Odlum ranch. Whenever the president visited, sometimes for weeks at the time, Jackie and Floyd also saw to it necessary arrangements were made for the president to have his support services, such as his secretary's services and separate phone lines. In 1961 the Eisenhowers, grandchildren and all, spent Christmas Eve there. The next day he wrote,

"Dear Jackie:
I can't tell you what a good time the Eisenhowers and the Gosdens had at your Christmas Eve party last evening. We are more than grateful to you and Floyd for taking us in, particularly since we represented a staggering number of bodies!

…On the way home all the children chattered incessantly about the exciting gifts they had received.

…Of course, for me personally one of the highlights of the evening was the special treat I had in watching you turn over the turkeys and making the gravy. I only wish that I could have been as expert in the carving department.

It was a lovely, happy and warm evening that we shall never forget. We are indebted to you and Floyd.

With affectionate regard,

D.E.

After Eisenhower's presidency, General Eisenhower and Mamie stayed in Jackie and Floyd's main guest cottage while deciding where to live. Eisenhower spent many months there working on his memoirs.

At Christmas, Aunt Jackie always sent our family fresh figs from the groves on her California ranch. She knew how much we had loved them when we lived there. Many Christmas cards with newsy notes are cataloged with her papers at the Dwight D. Eisenhower library in Abilene.

Jackie earned the life-long friendship of LBJ when she flew him from Dallas to the Mayo Clinic in Minnesota for emergency kidney-stone treatment. She had met Johnson earlier while working on a committee focusing on the new field of aviation medicine. Also Lyndon had helped Jackie work on the details for getting the 25 ATA women pilots to England during WWII.

In May of 1948 Senator Symington invited Jackie to a large luncheon supporting Johnson's run for the Senate, but when she got there Johnson was missing, as was his wife. Taking her aside, Symington told her Johnson was in a hospital nearby in terrible pain from kidney stone problems. They wanted to keep the news quiet, fearing it would hurt his campaign. She went to the hospital and found him in terrible shape. She knew a doctor at The Mayo Clinic who had had great success with a new type of kidney stone treatment, which did not require surgery and told the Johnsons about it. Within hours, Jackie had LBJ and Lady Bird aboard her Lodestar headed for Minnesota. Within seven days of the treatment Johnson was back on the campaign trail and went on to win by a narrow margin. He credited Jackie with saving his life.

In a biography of LBJ, Author Booth Mooney wrote: "Shortly after his opening campaign talk, Johnson captured the news headlines momentarily by coming down with a kidney infection and being dramatically flown by his friend, the famed Jacqueline Cochran, to the Mayo Clinic in Rochester, Minnesota, for treatment. He was there two weeks."

Another not-so-famous flight Jackie made to help someone was in 1956 when she flew her sister Mamie and Mamie's 18-year-old son, Jerry, to the Lovelace clinic for Mamie to have eye surgery. In a letter, Jackie explained to her friend Randy Lovelace, that Jerry and Mamie were part of the family who raised her, but she asked him not to mention this fact while they were there. On the other hand Jerry remembers how his Aunt Jackie made it clear they were not to discuss any family connections while they were at the clinic. Jackie flew them to the clinic in her ten-seat and paid for the operation.

Mamie and Myrtle's family stayed in California long after my father, mother, brothers and sisters had returned to Florida. Jackie and Floyd's main ranch had been finished and two of the guest cottages were complete when we left. Mamie's family moved into the ranch house we had lived in while we were there. Mamie's boys grew up on the ranch and worked for Jackie. Several family members still live in the area. When we all first got to Indio, it was just desert. Uncle Will Alford (Myrtle's husband) planted the first fruit trees at the ranch. Si Ingram, my mother's cousin, also came out from Florida and spent many years working with the orchard. It became an oasis. A paradise.

Jackie's efforts in working on other's campaigns were successful, but her foray into her own political campaigning wasn't. She declared herself Republican and in 1956 ran for the U.S. House of Representatives for California's 29th Congressional District seat. Her Democratic opponent Dalip Singh Saund, who came from India to the U. S. as a student and became a well-known businessman, and a district judge, beat her. An article in

Billie Pittman Ayers and Beth Dees

Time Magazine said Jackie had "long had a hankering to go to Congress," but personally, I think it was something Floyd wanted her to do rather it being something she wanted.

She campaigned valiantly nine months before the voting. She did manage to beat five male opponents in the primaries to gain the Republican Party nomination. Three weeks before the election President Eisenhower was in Los Angeles and invited her to come see him.

"Well, it's going to be awful nice to have you in Washington," he told her. Jackie then gave him a number of reasons she felt she was going to lose—by about 700 votes. Surprised, he said to send help with the campaigning. Jackie thanked him but said it was too late to do anything. She did indeed lose, by about 1,300 votes. President Eisenhower called twice a day after the election. Floyd accepted his calls because Jackie had left. She said, "I got into a corner and licked my wounds because it's no fun you know to spend nine months campaigning your heart out and then lose." Years later she would refer to the campaign as "very interesting…even though a little devastating."

After suffering one of the few defeats she had publicly experienced, Jackie turned away from politics, but not politicians. Two of the nation's top politicians—presidents—stopped in together to visit her one Sunday afternoon.

Jackie

"It happened on Sunday afternoon February, 1968, in the ranch house where my husband and I live nearby in Indio in the Southern California Desert. I doubt if

SUPERWOMAN Jacqueline Cochran

such a thing has happened before in the history of the United States.

A Democrat, Lyndon Baines Johnson, then President of the United States, and a Republican Dwight Eisenhower, former President of the United States jointly paid us a two-hour purely social call.

"President Johnson had flown out to San Diego the previous day to see a group of servicemen off for Vietnam. He came over Sunday morning to the desert to pay his respect to General Eisenhower. They had lunch together in the Eisenhower's winter home, a part of the Eldorado County Club about eight miles distance from our ranch. After lunch they played nine holes of golf but had one of the Secrete Service men call us to see if we were home and free to receive them. They would be over about 3 o' clock.

"It was well they called because with one exception we had let all the help off for the day! Floyd was not feeling too well and was still in bed and, while I was up, I had my hair in curlers. But one can do much in an hour and a half. They arrived with what looked like a double array of Secret Service men and we were prepared to receive them. Indeed I had rushed downtown to get a special low-calorie soft drink that I knew President Johnson liked. General Eisenhower had been in our rancho home many times. He first paid us a call when he was still president and while he did not know it, Floyd had just undergone a gall bladder operation at the Lovelace Clinic in Albuquerque, New Mexico, when he heard the president was going to call at our home. That's the way to get an operation fast because I flew Floyd home on the first post-operation day and we were there sitting on our lawn when the

Billie Pittman Ayers and Beth Dees

president and his friend George Allen arrived. But Floyd had with him his surgeon, the famous Randall Lovelace, who waited over until the next day to remove the stitches from the incision. After the General left office, he maintained his winter office in one of the guest cottages on our ranch until his last illness. Our living room has two original paintings by Dwight Eisenhower and eight mezzotints of his paintings, which he sent out as Christmas gifts to a small group of friends. One of the original painting is a portrait of Floyd painted as a birthday present to me in 1953. He later told me that to get it finished and to me by May 11th he used several of his lunch periods to paint.

"It was President Johnson's first visit to our ranch. They were received in our large living room. General Eisenhower took his spiked golf shoes off at the door and came into the room in his stocking fee. President Johnson had on his non-spike regular shoes.

"We showed the president the painting by General Eisenhower and the house, fed him a **dish of fresh dates and his favorite soft drink. Then after a general chat he said he wanted to see the ranch. The General stayed with Floyd while I took the wheel of the General's car and showed the president our date, tangerine and grapefruit groves and our public golf course. On the golf course I honked one couple aside and then stopped to apologize and asked them if they would like to meet the president of the United States. The wife apparently did not believe me, but the husband came over to the car and I guess received the surprise of his life because the president was really there and was very charming in his best Texas drawl. He was interested in seeing**

General Eisenhower's quarters, and I told him that was private and I did not go there except with his permission.

Fortunately the General's secretary was standing in front of her living quarters waiting for a glimpse of the president, so she took us into the office. It was there the General wrote most of his books and articles and carried on most of his conferences. It was a three-room **cottage overlooking a spacious lawn and then a grove of tangerines with the Santa Rosa Mountains about five miles beyond. The General loved it as his study retreat and told me that sometimes he would just sit and enjoy the view.... President Johnson was much taken by the General's office and asked me if I would do as much for him after he was out of office.**

"...Now why were a president and an ex-president so kind as to call on us that Sunday afternoon? I was very close to them both. ...I will just say that General Eisenhower gave me official credit for being one of few who convinced him he should seek the Presidency and I stood with him and Mamie on the rostrum at the convention in Chicago when he accepted the nomination. As for Lyndon Johnson, he has repeatedly said publicly that I saved his life. That is stretching the truth a bit, I think, but I certainly saved his career.

"It (the visit) represents one of the jewels of my mature life, but only one of the rarer of many jewels. I have known every president since Coolidge although I did not meet President Hoover until after he was out of office and I knew John Kennedy only casually. ...The lesson is that what I have done going from low to high, most anyone else can do if they are intelligent, ambitious and determined to go forward life."

Chapter Twelve: Yeager's mission: Save Jackie from Jackie

Chuck Yeager earned his place in history when he broke the speed of sound in 1947. His bravery, great eyesight and extraordinary piloting skills earned WWII ace Yeager the opportunity to fly through the sound barrier. Then a major in the United States Air Force—he laid many theories to rest, birthed a few new ones and wrote himself into the history books when he flew supersonic. Some of America's top flight engineers theorized his plane might explode on hitting the sonic barrier. Others believed the jet's tendency to vibrate roughly on approaching the speed of sound might shake it apart. It had happened before. Yeager and his plane sailed into the unknown, survived and became famous whether he wanted the national spotlight or not.

Yeager devoted a chapter in his first autobiography to Jackie. They played important roles in each other's lives. I first contacted General Yeager because he and Jackie were such good friends and he captured her personality better than I think anyone ever has when he said,

Chuck Yeager

"There weren't many like Jackie back in Hamlin [General Yeager's hometown], for sure. I never met anyone like her, man or woman. She came on like a human steamroller, and she'd take over your life if you let her. She was forever telling me how to talk and act, what tie to wear, what pants and jacket, what speeches to give and which to refuse. Hell, she would do that with

presidents. She'd read something in the papers about the Air Force or space program that she didn't like and pick up the telephone to call the White House. One time she didn't get through to Johnson. He called her back, but she told Floyd to tell LBJ she was washing her hair and for him to call back later. Floyd wanted to strangle her, but LBJ did call back."

General Yeager knew Jackie well, but he did not know about her childhood. "...Who knows all the things that happened to her growing up, she didn't talk about it much," he wrote in his book. In a phone interview he told my co-writer, "We did not stick our nose into each other's personal business ... and we didn't talk about 'surplus' subjects like childhood."

General Yeager and Jackie stood together many times to receive aviation awards and honors, one being the Harmon Trophies presented by President Eisenhower Nov. 17, 1954. Yeager and his wife, Glennis, spent many weekends at Jackie and Floyd's ranch. Here are a few stories from his book and an interview with him about Jackie:

Chuck Yeager

"... Jackie knew how to collect interesting people, and in her house we met African big-game hunters, dukes and duchesses, a Las Vegas casino owner, doctors, writers, movie stars, adventurers—even a Nevada sheriff. But what she liked most of all was to invite down a bunch of test pilots from Edwards (Air Force Base) and talk flying."

"...Jackie's record (breaking the sound barrier) was my project. I was her teacher and chase pilot. I first met her in 1947, not long after I broke the sound barrier, in Secretary of the Air Force Stuart Symington's office. She was a tall, blonde woman in her forties. 'I'm Jackie Cochran,' she said, pumping my hand. 'Great job, Captain Yeager. We're all proud of you.' She invited me to lunch, acting as if I should know exactly who she was, and caused an uproar just entering the posh Washington restaurant. The owner began bowing and scraping, and the waiters went flying. During the meal she sent back every other course, complaining loudly, and even marched into the kitchen to give the chef hell.

"In between pumping me for all the details of my X-1 flights, I learned a little about who she was. She was a honcho on several important aviation boards and committees and was a famous aviatrix before the war, winner of the Bendix air races; she had been a close friend of Amelia Earhart's. During the war she was...in charge of the WASP, the Women's Air Force Service Pilots ... Hell, she knew everybody and bounced all over the world: on VE Day, she was one of the first Americans to get down inside Hitler's bunker in Berlin, and came away with a gold doorknob off his bathroom by trading for it with a Russian soldier for a pack of Lucky Strikes. On VJ Day she was in Tokyo, playing poker with a couple of generals on MacArthur's staff and conned her way on board the battleship Missouri to watch the surrender ceremonies. As I would learn more than once over the next couple of decades, when Jackie Cochran set her mind to do something, she was a damned Sherman tank at full steam.

"We liked each other right off the bat ... She knew airplanes and said flat out that flying was the most important thing in her life. She was tough and bossy and used to getting her own way, but I figured that's how rich people behaved. When we parted that day she said, 'Let's stay in touch.' We sure did that. Glennis and I became Jackie and Floyd's closest friends. It was a friendship that lasted more than twenty-five years, until their deaths. I was the executor of Floyd's estate. They treated me like an adopted son. I flew around the world with Jackie, and she was right—she was a damned good pilot, one of the best. And I'm sure the reason she latched onto me was because for Jackie, nothing but the best would do, and she thought I was the best pilot in the Air Force. Hell, she'd say that to anybody, anytime."

General Yeager said straight out Jackie's money and powerful husband had a lot to do with her tremendous success. "Floyd…Mr. Odlum…was president of Canadair in Canada and they hired Jackie as a test pilot to fly the F-86 and she did a good job," he said. "…There were probably a lot of other ex-WASP who could have done just as good of a job if they had the experience Jackie had, but they didn't have the where-with-all to do it. She had connections and she used them."

Jackie made it her business to know generals, senators, and U.S. presidents. She worked at her friendships and she enjoyed them. She remembered birthdays with gifts, gave fabulous dinner parties and invited the powerful and highly visible to the comfortable refuge and warm hospitality of the Cochran-Odlum ranch in California. It didn't hurt that her Floyd was very wealthy and one of America's prominent industrialist. Jackie was an expert at many things, including making and keeping friends. Frequently those friendships yielded great opportunities that enabled her to make the flight that ensured her place in aviation history."

__Jackie__

"My husband had sold Consolidated Vultee Aircraft Company to General Dynamics Corporation, which had also other divisions, including the shipbuilding division and Canadair, in Canada (which built jets). Jay Hopkins was the leading spirit in General Dynamics Corporation and he was a great friend of John Mertz, who was a great friend of ours.

Jay Hopkins came to me early in 1953, or perhaps it was 1952, and asked me if I would like to fly their Canadian version of the F-86 for some records. It was to be powered with a new engine, produced in Canada, known as the Orenda and was supposed to have a little more speed than the North American's f-86. Of course I was delighted, and I suspected all along that perhaps John Mertz had something to do with this.

The schedule was set up, if possible to be carried out at Edwards Air Force Base, the U.S. base for experimental flying in California. I was to make arrangements for the use of that base, and they would bring the plane down from Canada for the purpose. First of all, I was to lay out a 100-kilometer circular course at Edwards Air Force Base, which cost on the order of $15,000. After that was laid out, it was difficult for the Secretary of Air not to allow me the use of that record course for this flying, even though it was a Canadian plane....

SUPERWOMAN Jacqueline Cochran

…. Chuck Yeager was chosen to serve as the chase pilot for these practice runs, and we established a very deep friendship that grew out of this set of records that I made. The practice runs perhaps utilized two to three weeks time in all and were done at all sorts of altitudes and speeds. The 100-kilometer record was then held by Fred Ascani, who was a friend of mine, and who is now a general in our Air Force. The records, itself, in those days had to be done at not to exceed 300 feet of altitude above the ground, because, in those days, they clocked around pylons, with a judge and a timer at each pylon, to see that you stayed on the outside of the circular course.

It was during the preliminaries for these record flights that I went through the sound barrier in the Canadian plane. In those days there was no plane, at least no military plane, or civil aviation plane that could beat the speed of sound in level flight. Chuck Yeager, in 1947, had done this in a very experimental plane, the X-1, which was powered with rockets and dropped out of another plane at an altitude of 45,000 feet. The only plane that could break the speed of sound, even in a direct full power dive was an F-86 and Chuck decided that I should have my wish to make the attempt. So he told me how to go about it and he flew his own plane up with me, to an altitude of something above 40,000 feet, where I turned over into a full powerful dive directly for the earth below…Chuck stayed up at that altitude until after I had come out of the dive about 15,000 to 18,000 feet above the ground. I had broken the sound barrier alright, but for some reason, the sound boom did not register on the instruments in the base and so I went up the next day, and did it again. It was an exciting experience, one of the most exciting experiences that I ever had in flying. In the first place the plane could not be stabilized. It would buck and kick, and veered back and forth and trembled and vibrated, all in a matter of seconds that was necessary to go above the speed of sound from above 45,000 to say 18,000 feet.

...There was a great feeling of speed that I first had in this Saberjet Canadian plane. Chuck and I would take off and, in a matter of minutes; we would be over the high Sierras...

...I, of course, thought that this was the ultimate in my flying experiences, and that my flying days were about over. I had broken the speed of sound, and I had flown a jet for the world's records. So it was then that I decided to write my book, "The Stars at Noon" and eventually to turn to other fields, particularly politics. I had flown for twenty years, and I did not realize at that time that I had so many more years still ahead of me. In any event I had far greater experiences in the Northrop T-38 and in the Lockheed-104."

On the morning of May 18, 1953, General Yeager considered it his military duty to keep his extraordinary eyesight on Jackie while they flew over the dry lakebeds near Edwards Air Force Base. "After only six or so flights in the Sabre, I figured she knew it well enough," Yeager said. "So I took her up to 45,000 feet and told her to push her nose straight down. We dove together, wing to wing, kept it wide opened and made a tremendous sonic boom above Edwards. She became the first woman to fly faster than sound, and forever after she loved to brag that she and I were the first and probably the last man and woman team to break Mach I together," he said.

Besides Floyd, General Yeager was probably one of the few people able to influence on Jackie. He tells a story about teaching Jackie how to tell time.

Chuck Yeager

"Jackie was to fly an F-86 at five in the morning. In the military when you say 5 o'clock, you mean 5 o'clock. Everything is geared to time. The first time Jackie was to fly an F-86 she showed up an hour later and I really landed on her hard with both feet. I said, 'Look if you are going to do this, you're going to be on time. You've got 25 guys out here trying to make this thing work for you and you come sauntering in an hour later. That's not the way it works in the military. She got a little huffy about that but she never did it again."

General Yeager accepted Jackie for who she was—rich, bossy, generous, charming and all the rest. He thought of Jackie as a pleasant-natured person—capable of great arrogance. Arrogance that on one occasion worked for her and on another created a fiasco.

In 1958, Jackie was elected the first female president of the Federation Aeronautique Internationale, the most prestigious aviation organization in the world. She was re-elected in 1959. She got permission from the military for General Yeager to fly with her to FAI's annual convention in Moscow. They traveled in Jackie's two-engine Lockheed Lodestar. The general wore civilian clothes and acted as Jackie's navigator and co-pilot. It was to be a three-week trip, but they weren't yet out of the country before they had their first adventure.

Chuck Yeager

"The Lodestar was a private, non-military plane but Jackie had obtained special permission from the Chief of Staff of the Air Force to stop at military bases along her route to refuel. It was 2 a.m., the gas tanks were running low and they decided to land at a base in Presque Isle, Maine. Evidently not everyone got the word about Jackie coming through because when Yeager radioed in for permission to land, the tower refused to give it, even when he told them Jackie had special permission. "Yeah, so does Lana Turner," came the reply.

"Jackie had had enough. Jackie grabbed the mike. 'This is Jacqueline Cochran. I am landing.' As soon as we stopped rolling, the airplane was surrounded by air police, who clomped aboard, ordered us out, and escorted us under guard to base operations. Finally the base commander arrived, a bird colonel who obviously didn't read his mail, because Jackie's name meant nothing to him. 'You people will leave immediately,' he said. 'This base is closed to all civilian traffic.' I just waited for Jackie to blow, but she surprised me by smiling sweetly and asking, 'Sir, may I have your permission to make a phone call?' The colonel nodded and Jackie began to dial. It was two-thirty in the morning. She said, 'Tommy, sorry to wake you, but I've just landed at your base at Presque Isle, and I'm getting the idiot's treatment. Yes sir, he's standing right here.' She handed the receiver to the colonel. He was the first guy I ever saw talk on the phone while standing at attention. His face turned to chalk, and he muttered, "Yes, sir" over and over as he got Roto-Rootered long distance by the Chief of Staff. When he hung up, he managed a small smile and said to Jackie,

'Miss Cochran, you can have anything you need or want, including this air base.'"

About a dozen countries were represented at the FAI convention, which lasted a week. Jackie was where she loved to be, running the show. It was, of course, a success, but it took its toll on Jackie's patience. It was a different culture, a different way of doing things and Jackie's standard of perfection created stress for everyone around her and for herself. It became apparent she was fresh out of charm one night on their flight home when she and Yeager attended a dinner party in Bulgaria.

"We were coming home from Russia," Yeager said. "We flew down to Bulgaria ... that evening we had dinner with a Bulgarian air marshal. Jackie was telling him her plans. This general told her the Turks won't let anybody fly in from Bulgaria because they hate each other's guts. She said, 'What do you mean I can't go to Turkey?' She picks up a phone and gets her little black book out and in about two minutes she's talking to the chief of staff of Turkey's Air Force, telling him, 'I've got this idiot general here, who's telling me I can't fly into Turkey. Would you give me permission?' And boy, this general—who unfortunately understood English very well—put his hand...his finger on the phone cradle and said, 'Miss Cochran, you've got one hour to get out of Bulgaria and you're going through Yugoslavia.' I just looked at Jackie and said, 'Jackie, you're a damn fool.'"

"...She knew she had made a very big mistake. You could tell she was sorry and she kind of mulled about it all the way to Spain...but she wasn't the kind of person to waste time crying over spilt milk. She realized she made a big mistake, she registered it and that was it."

Jackie's strong personality made her wonderful friends and powerful enemies. Her loyalty to Yeager was as strong as her connection to the Air Force. She was involved in the beginnings of the U.S. Air Force when it became a separate branch of the armed forces. The Air Force's loyalty was returned and it honored her often for her accomplishments and patriotism. In 1969 she was awarded the Distinguished Flying Cross and the next year she received the Legion of Merit. In 1970 she retired as a full colonel in the Air Force Reserves. Among her collections of trophies and gifts, she was particularly proud of a saber presented to her by the cadets at the U.S. Air Force Academy. She requested to be buried with it.

In 1960, at an age when many women might be slowing down, Jackie continued at supersonic speed. At age 54, she became the first woman to fly Mach2, twice the speed of sound. She rewrote aviation's record books in the next couple of years. Flying an F-104 Starfighter, which General Yeager described as "intimidating" to many experienced jet pilots, Jackie set 69 inter-city and straight-line distance jet records and nine international speed, distance and altitude jet records.

Jackie

"The fact is that I flew this powerful fighter plane (Lockheed 104 Jet "Starfighter) a distance more than around the world at the equator while preparing for these three record attempts. Some of the flights were thoroughly to familiarize myself with the flight characteristics of the plane. Some were practice flights over the courses with only the moving picture cameras mounted in the cockpit to give me the mach number I

had reached and the temperature in the jet engine inlet...Under the International regulations, you first have to get permission for the record flights and for this a substantial fee must be paid. Then after the judges have made up all the documents and certified the flight as a record to the national organization representing the Federation Aeronautique Internationale (in our case the National Aeronautic Association) you have one week to do it over without payment of another fee.

"... While I have never read anything that has appeared in the press about me, my husband tells me that there was hardly a line about my Starfighter flights. I flew that F-104 G Starfighter faster that it had ever been flown before by any man or woman. My flights enabled the planes at the General Electric jet power plan to be re-evaluated so as to give it more operational maximum speed. That was the purpose of the flights and the mission was accomplished. That I, a woman, did this gave some accent to the accomplishment. There are several jet test pilots I know who could have done as well. But they could not have done any better because I got the maximum out of the plane & power plan that the technicians had worked out as possible.

I got more speed than any one had got before, only because the Lockheed people and General Electric Company agreed in advance that I could put the engine to temperatures previously prohibited by the operating manuals. ...Cameras in the cockpit kept a record of the reading of each instrument... The public knew little about these flights."

There is no doubt in my mind Jackie ever tired of her fame, or ever stopped missing her family. She loved the speed of the jets, the finest of silks, the best of company and the bustle of activity of living a full life.

Jackie

"The demands on my time are almost overwhelming. Sometimes I think I would like to run away from it all and hide. But I guess if the requests for speeches, public appearances, letters, pictures and autographs were to ease I might feel forgotten and somewhat unhappy. As it is, I have two secretaries ... on my regular payroll and sometimes must bring in extra temporary help...My telephone bill usually runs to several hundred dollars per month and my travel expenses to meet the commitments I have made are heavy. I try to do most of my domestic traveling in my own plane. It carries ten passengers. ...

...There is a great diversity as to the things and I am asked to do and the substance of the letters received. This morning's mail, before me now, includes the following:

-A letter from the Right Honorable Lord Casey of Canberra, Australia about a Spanish boy I had educated and then sent to Australia to get a start in life.

-A letter from the head of Girls Town Foundation asking permission to use my voice recording for a movie they are making.

-A letter from D. Geranopoulos of the Aero Club of Greece asking me to a September aviation meeting...

-A letter from Senator Howard Cannon discussing my air feats, the Bendix Air Race, etc.

SUPERWOMAN Jacqueline Cochran

-A letter from the head of the Air Museum at the Smithsonian Institution about a permanent panel or showcase that is to be dedicated to me.
-A letter from Dr. Edward Teller asking me to dinner with him and Mrs. Teller on May 25.

Chuck Yeager said Jackie used to boast they were probably the first and last man and woman to break the sound barrier together.

Chapter Thirteen: Smooth Landings

Jackie's last flight was in the Paris Air Show in the summer of 1971. She thought the chest pains she experienced while there signaled pneumonia so she tried to slow down and rest when she got home. The pains continued. Later trips to the doctor revealed she had atrial fibrillation, a condition I've been diagnosed with also, which causes a spasm in the heart muscle and inefficient blood circulation. My sister Gwen died from emphysema and a similar heart condition. My father also died with heart problems.

Placed on medication, Jackie realized with great sadness her flying days might be over. One day she fainted at home. Surgery followed and she received a pacemaker, then another and then another over the next few years. Jackie was grounded.

She told an Indio reporter in 1973, "It's sad and difficult to talk about flying…for a long time I couldn't look at a plane without bursting into tears."

She did look into getting her glider pilot's license in 1974, but didn't follow through.

In 1972, she and Floyd sold their ranch in a multi-million dollar deal to Odlum Corporation that was managed by Floyd's son, Bruce. The next January, they moved into a new, modest ranch home, adjoining the ranch property. The original ranch house was converted into the Coachella Valley Country Club, and later the Indian Palms Country Club. The surrounding acreage became home sites for a $100 million dollar residential development. Only one room, called the Eisenhower Room, remains standing today after the main ranch burned in the early 1990s in a fire some think vandals set.

Floyd died at age 80 in 1977. He and Jackie had been married 41 years. He did not want a headstone or burial services. Floyd was indeed a humble man. Jackie adored him. We admired him. As Floyd requested, General Yeager, executor of Floyd's estate, flew over the ranch to scatter his ashes. From the first time we met Floyd in 1935, my family always appreciated his great love for Jackie. We also admired him because, like Jackie, he was an exceptional person.

Jackie's health began declining rapidly after Floyd's death. Yeager was one of the few to continue to go out and visit Jackie.

Glennis [General Yeager's wife] said of Jackie's last years,

"I think she just gave up and wanted out. She suffered heart and kidney failure, became swollen and had to sleep sitting up in a chair. It got to the point where friends didn't want to visit her because she became so impossible. Chuck continued to visit and was about the only one on earth who could get her to smile."

Getting old was about the only thing Jackie didn't figure out how to get around. Used to getting her way, wrinkles and pacemakers were never on her agenda. Perhaps the reason she never adapted gracefully to her wheelchair had to do with her life-long habit of flying fast jets, setting world records, buying fashions fresh from Paris, directing an international cosmetics firm, being close friends with presidents, generals, movie stars and other famous people—in other words effecting history.

SUPERWOMAN Jacqueline Cochran

Jackie did not let death creep up and catch her disorganized. Famous for detailed planning, she didn't forget to plan her funeral and have her affairs in order. By1977, Jackie had sold the house and lot she owned in DeFuniak Springs to local resident, Angus "Hank" Douglass and his wife. Aunt Myrtle had lived there before she died. In a 1964 letter to her realtor, Burl Underwood, she insisted the house be torn down before the property was sold. It was done. She attended the details for cemetery plots other than just her own. Jackie owns a plot for the Pittman family in the Magnolia Cemetery in DeFuniak Springs, the town where I was born and the town where she spent many years, some difficult ones. About a year before Jackie's death, new headstones were placed on the graves of Jackie's parents—Mollie and Ira Pittman. No one in the family still living knows who did it. I believe she, or maybe someone representing her wishes, had the headstones upgraded and taken care of. Her own child's original small heart-shaped headstone, black with age and grown over with lichen, remained untouched. Perhaps that memory was too painful and had been buried long ago.

Jackie was not afraid of much in life and I never heard her talk about death. She was more afraid of the possibility of pain, disfiguring injuries or the damage to a plane from a crash. To her, dying was simply as a step in the soul's progression, no different than eating or sleeping.

The last family member to visit Jackie before she died was Gwen. In March of 1980, she and her husband, A.E. "Bud" Ericson flew from their home in Prattville, Ala. to California to see Jackie. She said of the trip, "Bud and I flew out with the sole purpose of seeing her one last time because we knew she was very ill. She was very gracious and I wouldn't take anything for that visit. It was Bud's first time to meet Jackie and having been a military man, he told her how as a young air traffic controller at the Orlando airport, he remembered the "boys in the tower" talking about Jackie winning the Bendix.

She may have been near death and very ill at the time, but Jackie's ego was eternal and still stopped Bud mid-conversation to correct him. "My boy, I won two Bendix trophy races," she said firmly.

Gwen, who looked like Jackie in her early teenage years and in her late life years, also had her same air of elegant reserve and steeliness on occasion. In the early 1950's Gwen found herself invited to a social affair in Miami where Jackie was to be the guest speaker. She contacted Jackie beforehand and discussed the upcoming event. "I would like to come hear you," she told Jackie. "But I don't want to embarrass you. By the same token I don't want to be embarrassed either." This gentle request evidently didn't register with Jackie because she proceeded to tell the audience her usual spiel about starting out as a poor orphan. They met afterwards, and Gwen didn't comment on the speech but she did say, "I wish my sons had the opportunity to know you better," to which Jackie replied. "Well, why not?"

"Because you're too damn hard to explain," Gwen told her, turned and walked away. Even though she was proud of her aunt, Gwen never capitalized on being related to a celebrity or bragged about their kinship. Though they were close when Gwen was young, as the years went by—particularly after our mother died—Gwen and Jackie talked less and less. "We did stay in touch over the years. It was simple. I would call her now and then and she would call me," Gwen said.

SUPERWOMAN Jacqueline Cochran

Jackie's funeral service, conducted by Father Charles Depiere, was simple, and dignified. Charles Depiere had known Jackie for the past 25 years and arrived at her bedside in time to administer the last Catholic rites before her death. Only thirteen individuals, including Yeager and Ann Wood-Kelly among her old friends, were asked to attend the private graveside service near Jackie's home in Indio, California. Jackie could have afforded a casket to rival a queen's but, she wanted to go back into the earth as "food for the daisies," she once told Floyd. She asked to be buried in a simple wooden coffin. When I went to ceremony in California where the U.S Postal Service honored her with an air mail stamp bearing her likeness I stopped to visit her grave. It is a simple, flat marble marker surrounded by green grass. She would have been pleased.

Four months later a memorial was held for her at the U.S. Air Force Academy in Colorado Springs. She is the only woman to have her memorabilia on permanent display at the museum.

She willed most of what was left of her estate to the United States Air Force to be used for research projects. This was further testament to her patriotism and desire to add to a knowledge base. Family members were included in her will.

Despite what I know and what I've learned, it is not easy to understand why someone who dealt with life in so forthright a manner would deny such a vital part of it—family. Was her ambition so strong, it included an image, once built, had to be maintained, no matter how high the costs to her relationship with her family? Did she believe her own story in the end? Our family did not deny or ignore the life story she told the public.

Billie Pittman Ayers and Beth Dees

Aunt Jackie was a young woman when she first made the statement to the press about being an orphan. Perhaps she thought the sympathy might draw more attention. In a way, it wasn't important—what she said. She was my aunt, we knew she was famous and we were proud for her. It was easy to love her wonderful qualities. I wasn't even aware until I became much older of things she said regarding the family and her early life because I was busy taking care of my own family of two children and a husband who kept us on the move with his military career.

My mother believed Aunt Jackie created her early life story for Floyd's sake. Mother felt Jackie might have felt if Floyd knew the truth in the early delicate stage of their relationship he might reject her. In those years her divorce and the affair with a married man would have been frowned on. Why she told such a story is complex and leaves questions. To me it is still sad, she seemed to reinvent her childhood to fill her needs, putting her pride above family, and never set the record straight. She is human as I am human. Her shadows will never diminish the bright shining person she was. It will never dull her family's love for her.

Among Jackie's papers at the Eisenhower Library in Abilene, Kansas is a response from the U.S. Census Bureau to Jackie's request for her personal census information in the year 1920. She requested the search be done in the name of "Jacqueline Cochran". Not surprisingly, the paperwork said, "No results." What if she had given her real birth name of 'Bessie Lee Pittman'? She once hired a personal detective to research her background. She did give him her correct birth date. She did tell him her birthplace was in Northwest Florida but she failed to give him the fact of her real name being Bessie Pittman. Expectedly, he too, came up empty-handed. Despite my admiration for her accomplishments as an aviatrix, and my love for her as my aunt, I would not be surprised at what she might have done to prevent her story from being challenged. She had an image to protect...at all costs.

Thomas Branigar, archivist at the Dwight d. Eisenhower Library, Abilene, Kansas, worked for seven years, nine months cataloging Jackie's papers after her death. There are 365 file cabinet size boxes in the collection making hers' the fourth largest collection there. When Branigar finished, he wrote an introduction to the collection stating, "Jacqueline Cochran, cosmetics executive and world-famous aviatrix...Born Bessie Pittman about 1906 in Northwest Florida, she was the youngest of five children of Ira and Mary (Grant) Pittman." As I've stated earlier, Ira and Mary were my grandparents.

In 1996, I was invited by Shutsy Reynolds, a former WASP, to attend the WASP dinner and First Day of Issue stamp ceremony in Indio, California and a memorial service honoring Jackie with a commemorative 50 cents air mail stamp bearing her likeness. These women, who so admired what Jackie had done during her lifetime, campaigned diligently to see the stamp added to a series honoring our country's greats. Shutsy, who runs a store of WASP memorabilia, is a sunny, friendly person and she introduced me around with great enthusiasm as Jackie's niece. It was an honor to meet and talk with several of the WASPs. My cousin, Tom Alford, and his wife, Louise, attended the events with me.

The ceremony was held on the site of the Cochran-Odlum ranch, the ranch my father helped build in 1935. I felt overwhelmed, by memories from 60 years earlier. Driving through the area, smelling the sweet fragrance of the orchid trees I recalled Aunt Jackie's love for beautiful surroundings and felt a great appreciation for the Garden of Eden she and Floyd had created. The next morning we attended a memorial service, sponsored by the WASP, held at the Coachella Valley Cemetery, where Jackie is buried. I felt great happiness to be there, witnessing this great honor bestowed on my Aunt Jackie.

On November 17, 1992 Aunt Jackie was inducted into the Florida Women's Hall of Fame, founded by then-Senator Robert Graham. I was asked to accept the plaque on Jackie's behalf. My daughter, Vicki and two nieces, Sharon and Carolyn attended the ceremony with me at the Governor's Mansion in Tallahassee. It was gratifying to have her home state honor her in this way. Two years later, a photograph and information about her and those of the other inductees were placed on permanent display in the state capitol's rotunda.

News of the death of the famous aviatrix flew around the world when Aunt Jackie died August 9, 1980 at her home from a heart attack. Despite many discrepancies regarding her age and birthplace, obituaries like the following, covered many accurate accountings of her tremendous accomplishments; organizing the WASP, being the first woman to break the sound barrier and her record of aviation records.

"Jacqueline Cochran, the first woman pilot to break the sound barrier and matriarch of the Women's Air Force Service Pilots in World War II, died in her sleep Saturday at 74"

She set world speed and altitude records, was the first woman to pilot a bomber across the North Atlantic (in June 1941), was awarded the Clifford Burke Harmon trophy about 15 times as outstanding woman flier of the world, and became the first living woman to be enshrined in the Aviation Hall of Fame (1971)."

Many of the obituaries included her rags-to-riches story about her being an orphan with nothing and climbing up to the stars. So much of it is true. Jackie was truly great...to the world ...and to me. My single wish is that it be known that Jackie—Bessie Pittman—was born into our family and shared in our love for each other.

Billie Pittman Ayers and Beth Dees

Bibliography By Chapter

Chapter One

Interview with Columbia University. Cochran Collection in Dwight D. Eisenhower Library in Abilene, Kansas.

Ovanin, Sara A. "History of Bagdad," *The Press-Gazette*, Milton, Florida, June 24, 1965.

Yeager, Chuck and Charles Leerhsen, *Press On!* New York: Bantam Books, 1988.

Cochran, Jacqueline, article draft for *Time Magazine*. Unpublished. Cochran Collection, DDE Library.

Ayers, Billie P. Personal Papers.

Thirteenth Census of the United States (1910).

The Mobile Press-Register, June 21, 1941.

Interview with Nellie Peagler Bowman, Erma Peagler's daughter, August 8, 1996.

Interview with Harold Gillis, local historian of DeFuniak Springs. Spring, 1998.

Elliott, James *History of the Lumber Industry in Northwest Florida*. In collection at University of West Florida.

Interview with Paula Mundy in Jacksonville office of Social Services Administration.

Cochran, Jacqueline, draft from *More Stars of Noon* manuscript, Cochran Collection at DDE Library.

"Mother of Aviatrix Interview" *Pensacola News-Journal*, re-printed in the *Indio News*, June 30, 1939.

Chapter Two

Willis, Elaine C. and Toifel, Peggy W. and Wolfe, Lea, *We Remember Bagdad,* St. Augustine: Southern Heritage Press, 1992.

Cochran, Jacqueline draft from *More Stars at Noon* manuscript, Cochran Collection at DDE Library.

Interview with Bagdad, Florida resident Rubin Smith, 1995.

Interview Bagdad, Florida resident Anice Presley Smith, 1995.

Chapter Three

Fourteenth Census of the United State of America (1920).

Rolfsen, Bruce "Paxton Survives Test of Time To Become Thriving Community" *Our Town*, published by The Northwest Florida Daily News, 1992.

Marriage license of Bessie Pittman and Robert Cochran, Blakley, Georgia courthouse.

Thompson, Ina, "History of Walton County" *The DeFuniak Springs Herald-Breeze*, June 24, 1970.

Interview with Noma, Florida native Lutrell Hinote, 1981.

Huyck, Tom "The Secret of Lakewood Has Not Yet Been Revealed" *Our Town* published by The Northwest Florida Daily News, 1992.

Interview with Freeport resident, Lucy Marse, March 1995.

Armstrong, Clay H. (Professor) *History of Escambia County, Florida*, St. Augustine: The Record Company, 1930. From the collection of University of West Florida.

Court records in Walton County, Nov.25, 1926.

Interview with DeFuniak Springs resident "Weba" Paul, May, 1995.

Interview with Niceville resident Bill Meigs, August 1994.

Interview with DeFuniak Springs resident and historian Jeanette McDonald.

Interview with DeFuniak Springs resident and historian Howard Nowling, Nov. 1994.

Interview with DeFuniak Springs resident Hank Douglass, 1995.

Interview with DeFuniak Springs resident Mrs. Maude Mayo, May 1996.

Interview with Cecil "Wendy" Neel and Sybil Neel, Aug., 1995.

Dooley, Sharon "Meigs Family was known for political clout" *The Bay Beacon*, April 19,1995.

Interview with DeFuniak Springs resident Elizabeth Neel. Nov.,1997.

Interview with Niceville resident, Bill Meigs, 1995.

Reardon, Anna, "Jacqueline Cochran" The DeFuniak Springs Herald-Breeze, Sept. 4, 1980.

Interview with Phil Harris, Aug., 1995.

Chapter Four

"Five Year Old Child is Fatally Burned Friday" *The Breeze,* June 4, 1925.

Taped interview with Billie Ayers, Gwen Erickson, Hubert 'Pinkie' Grant, Dec., 7, 1980.

"San Carlos...The Memories Linger" *Pensacola Magazine*, April 1993.

Interview with DeFuniak resident Phil Harris, April 1996.

Brown, Warren J. *Florida's Aviation History: The First One Hundred Years*, Second Edition, Largo Florida: Aero-Medical Consultants Inc. 1994.

Associated Press "West Florida Man is Among Four Drowned" *The Breeze*, Nov. 8, 1930.

Chapter Five

Interview with Ponce de Leon residents Ed and Nettie Mae Rushing, April 1996.

Interview with DeFuniak Springs resident, Mary Caroline Murray, 1996.

Interview with Ruby Burton, 1994.

Chapter Six

"Odlum will accepted by court in probate action" *Riverside Enterprise* Aug. 23, 1976.

"A Financier with the Midas Touch" newspaper article in family collection, dated Jan. 2.

"Wright, Robert A., "Floyd Odlum and the Work Ethic" *The New York Times*, Jan. 28, 1973.

Inscription to Jackie from Floyd in journal he gave her. In Scrapbook Series in DDE Library.

Porter, Sylvia "Double Success Story" *New York Post* as printed in *Look Magazine* April 12, 1949.

Chapter Seven

Cochran, Jacqueline "Grooming is a Breeze, Says High-Flying Jackie" Washington D.C. Times-Herald, 1953.

Yeager, Chuck and Leo Janos, *Yeager*, Bantam Books, New York, July 1985.

Chapter Eight

Barton, Charles "Jackie and the Bendix" *Air Classics* May 1985.

Taves, Isabella "Lady in a Jet" *The Reader's Digest* Aug., 1955.

Cochran, Jacqueline, Cochran Collection at DDE Library.

"But $5,500 Means Little to Jacqueline These Days" *Voice of the People*, Sept. 10, 1937.

"And Miss Cochrane Has Some of 'Em Burned Up." *Voice of the People* September 16, 1938.

"DeFuniak Woman Wins Bendix Derby" *Voice of the People*, Sept. 9, 1938.

Aviation History Magazine July 1997.

Barton, Charles "Jackie & The Bendix" *Air Classics* May. 1985.

Chapter Nine

Cochran, Jacqueline, "Sixth Sense" *Vogue Magazine*, Sept. 15, 1954.

Cochran, Jacqueline "The Amelia I Knew" *Ninety-Nines Magazine*, 1949.

Typed Interview with Jackie and Floyd Odlum [General Collection] Box 233,
Cochran Collection at DDE Library.

Eickman, Pat "Jackie Cochran: on her friend and herself" *The Enterprise and The Press*, Feb. 1, 1978.

Interview with Columbia University. Cochran Collection in DDE Library.

Lovell, Mary S. *Straight On 'Til Morning: The biography of Beryl Markam*. New York, St. Martin's Press. 1987.

Rich, Doris L. *Amelia: A Biography* Smithsonian Institution, 1989.

Chapter Ten

"WASPs Made Eligible" *Congress and the Nation*, Vol. V.

Cochran, Jacqueline, Article Final Draft "Men May Own Big Business But They Rely On Women To Run Them" for Business and Professional Women's Club, 1957.

Verges, Marianne *On Silver Wings*, Ballantine Books, 1991.

Granger, Byrd Howell *On Final Approach: The Women Air force Service Pilots* of World War II. Scottdsdale, AZ Falconer Publishing Company 1991.

Darr, Ann "*The Women Who Flew—But Kept Silent.*" *The New York Times Magazine,* May 7, 1985.

Deactivation Letter to WASPs from Jackie in file from Maxwell Air Force Base/Historical Research Center in Montgomery, Alabama.

Speech by Ann Wood-Kelly Mar., 9 1996 at Cochran Stamp Ceremony in California.

Cochran, Jackie. Draft for second autobiography. Cochran Collection, DDE Library.

Wester, Michael O. "Flying WASP meet again" *Press Enterprise*, June 18, 1972.

Cochran, Jacqueline, "Women in Space" *Parade Magazine*, April 30, 1961.

Weatherford, Doris *American Women in World War II*, Facts On File, 1990.

Battelle, Phyllis "Why Not Women in Outer Space?" *San Francisco News Call Bulletin*,
July 24, 1962.

"America's Space Program Open to Women" Public Service Announcement from NASA Vol.1, No. 2. May 1, 1963.

Memorandum to Mr. Webb and Dr. Dryden on file with NASA, July 26.

Congressional Record of the 84th Congress, June 13, 1955.

Report on the Committee on Science and Astronautics before the U.S. House of Representatives for 87th Congress, Second Session.

Chapter Eleven

Yeager, Chuck and Leo Janos, *Yeager*, Bantam Books, New York, July 1985.

"Jackie and the Judge" *Time Magazine*, Oct. 8, 1956.

"Political Notes" *Time Magazine*, Jan. 9, 1956.

"Cochran's Airborne Campaign" *Life Magazine*. 1956.

Western Union Telegram from President Dwight D. Eisenhower Nov. 7, 1956.

Letter from President Dwight D. Eisenhower, Aug. 13, 1956.

Letter from President Dwight D. Eisenhower Dec. 25, 1961.

Chapter Twelve

Yeager, Chuck and Leo Janos, *Yeager*, Bantam Books, New York, July 1985.

Cochran Collection at DDE Library.

Chapter Thirteen

"Jacqueline Cochran Dies; Record-Shattering Pilot" *Los Angeles Times* Aug. 10, *1980*.

Will of Jacqueline Cochran, filed for probate Sept. 22, 1980. Copy on file at Walton County courthouse in Florida.

Record of Burials, Magnolia Cemetery, DeFuniak Springs, Florida.

Warranty Deed between Jacqueline Cochran Odlum and Angus G. Douglass and wife, Hope H. Douglass. Copy on file at Walton County courthouse in Florida.

Other References

Yeager, Chuck and Leo Janos, *Yeager*, Bantam Books, New York, July 1985.

Brinley, Maryann Bucknum and Jacqueline Cochran *Jackie Cochran: The Autobiography of the Greatest Woman Pilot in Aviation History*. Bantam Books. August 1987.

McGuire, Nina and Sandra Wallus Sammons, *Jacqueline Cochran: America's Fearless Aviator*. Lake Buena Vista, Florida. Tailored Tours Publications. 1997.

Weatherford, Doris *American Women and World War II*, New York, Facts on File 1990.

United States Air Force Historical Division. Chronology of American Aviation 1903-1953, Pamphlet No. 210-1-1. Department of the Air Force. July 1955.

Cochran, draft from More Stars At Noon (unpublished) in Cochran collection at DDE Library.

Cochran, Jacqueline, *Stars At Noon* Atlantic Monthly: Little, Brown and Company, 1954.

Texas University Library
Franklin D. Roosevelt Library

Dwight D. Eisenhower Library
Ayers, Billie P. Personal Papers.

Ladevich, Laurel, Writer, Producer and Director for Documentary "The American Experience: Fly Girls" Public Broadcasting Service, June 2001.

About The Authors

In her hometown of DeFuniak Springs, Florida, as a teenager Beth Dees first heard stories from old timers about a local woman, Bessie Pittman, who had changed her name to Jackie Cochran and become famous internationally, primarily as a pilot. She was struck by the disparities between the local's stories and the woman's autobiography. Dees reported for daily newspapers for years after earning her journalism degree from Auburn University in Alabama and later worked in public relations for resorts and an electric utility. Publishing her first news article in 1976, she began freelancing full-time in 1997. Twenty-three years later, she writes full-time for magazines, web sites, commercial clients and non-profit organizations. In 1998, she published a non-fiction book on Christmas collectibles.

In 1994, Dees met Billie Pittman Ayers, who explained her family had wanted to write about Bessie Pittman/Jacqueline Cochran since around 1980. Mrs. Ayers spent years, helping Dees with the research, writing and gathering information from other family members about her aunt. Sadly on August 15, 1999 Mrs. Ayers died from a stroke. It was her wish this story be published to help historians or others interested in Jackie's life. She also felt it was important to "Set the record straight," for the family.

Printed in the United States
3497